BLACK

INDIANS

A HIDDEN HERITAGE

BOOKS BY WILLIAM LOREN KATZ

The Black West: A Documentary and Pictorial History of the African American Role in the Westward Expansion of the United States

Black Indians: A Hidden Heritage

The Cruel Years: American Voices at the Dawn of the Twentieth Century

The Lincoln Brigade: A Picture History

Black Pioneers: An Untold Story

Black Legacy: A History of New York's African Americans

Flight from the Devil: Six Slave Narratives

Black Women of the Old West

Eyewitness: A Living Documentary of the African American Contribution to American History

Proudly Red and Black: Stories of African and Native Americans

A History of Multicultural America series (eight volumes)

Black People Who Made the Old West

Breaking the Chains: African-American Slave Resistance

The Invisible Empire: The Ku Klux Klan Impact on History

An Album of Nazism

An Album of the Great Depression

Minorities in American History series (six volumes)

An Album of the Civil War

An Album of Reconstruction

The Constitutional Amendments

A History of Black Americans

Teaching Black History in the Classroom

Black Studies Resources and User's Guide

American Majorities and Minorities: A Syllabus of United States History for Secondary Schools

Teachers' Guide to American Negro History

INDIANS

BLACK

A HIDDEN HERITAGE

WRITTEN BY WILLIAM LOREN KATZ

ATHENEUM BOOKS FOR YOUNG READERS
NEW YORK LONDON TORONTO SYDNEY NEW DELHI

ATHENEUM BOOKS FOR YOUNG READERS
An imprint of Simon & Schuster Children's Publishing Division
1230 Avenue of the Americas, New York, New York 10020
Copyright © 1986 by Ethrac Publications, Inc.
All rights reserved, including the right of reproduction in whole
or in part in any form.
ATHENEUM BOOKS FOR YOUNG READERS is a registered
trademark of Simon & Schuster, Inc.
For information about special discounts for bulk purchases,
please contact Simon & Schuster Special Sales at 1-866-506-1949
or business@simonandschuster.com.
The Simon & Schuster Speakers Bureau can bring authors to
your live event. For more information or to book an event, contact
the Simon & Schuster Speakers Bureau at 1-866-248-3049 or
visit our website at www.simonspeakers.com.
Also available in an Atheneum Books for Young Readers
hardcover edition
Book design by Debra Sfetsios-Conover
The text for this book is set in Adobe Caslon.
Manufactured in the United States of America
This Atheneum Books for Young Readers paperback edition
January 2012
20 19 18 17 16 15 14 13
The Library of Congress has cataloged the hardcover edition
as follows:
Katz, William Loren.
Black Indians.
Bibliography: p. 191.
Includes index.
Summary: Traces the history of relations between blacks and
American Indians, and the existence of black Indians, from the
earliest foreign landings through pioneer days.
1. Afro-Americans—Relations with Indians—Juvenile literature.
2. Indians of North America—Mixed bloods—Juvenile literature.
[1. Afro-Americans—Relations with Indians. 2. Indians of North
America—Mixed bloods.] I. Title.
E98.R28K37
1986
970.004'043
85-25770
ISBN 978-1-4424-4636-6 (hc)
ISBN 978-1-4424-4637-3 (pbk)

To friends Jean Carey Bond, Osceola Townsend, George Tooks, Pompey Fixico, and Woody Strode, and their heroic ancestors, the heroes of this book. And to Kenneth Wiggins Porter— forerunner, scholar, mentor—who embraced the creed lived by Wild Cat and John Horse: love of people and resistance to tyranny.

—W. L. K.

THE EUROPEAN is to the other races of mankind what man himself is to the lower animals: he makes them subservient to his use and when he cannot subdue he destroys them.

Alexis de Tocqueville, *Democracy in America*, 1835

ONE OF THE LONGEST unwritten chapters in the history of the United States is that treating of the relations of the Negroes and the Indians. The Indians were already here when the white men came and the Negroes brought in soon after to serve as a subject race found among the Indians one of their means of escape.

Carter G. Woodson, *Journal of Negro History*, 1920

IN THE COURSE OF TIME the American people got into Florida and began to live. This caused trouble. The colored people and the Indians, being natives of the land, naturally went on the warpath. They fought until the American people called for peace. The Indians and the Negroes gave them peace.

Joe Philips, Black Seminole, 1930

⇥ CONTENTS ⇤

PREFACE TO THE TWENTY-FIFTH ANNIVERSARY EDITION

WHEN *BLACK INDIANS* APPEARED a quarter of a century ago, it was ignored by the mainstream media but triggered immediate, full-throated, multilayered and louder public responses than my forty other books. It won no prizes but was hawked by street booksellers in Manhattan from 8th Street and Sixth Avenue to 125th Street and in other cities.

However, for white people, the book's title and cover immediately stirred controversy that still continues to this day. So many expressed annoyance with the title, I wondered if any bothered to open the book. While reading it on New York subways, WLIB radio talk show host Imotep Gary Byrd was confronted by white riders who pointed to the cover and title and heatedly said, "There were *not!*" When his son brought a copy to his social studies teacher, he met "Oh come on!" disbelief.

Some reacted negatively before the book appeared. One New York Native American Nation denied me permission to use a 1940s group photo of their members . . . in a book entitled *Black*

Indians. When I showed this picture to an African American friend, he recognized his uncle and then identified half of the other figures as descended from Africans.

Some responses were far from painless. After some university and museum lectures, students of color approached me in tears. A young woman at John Jay College said, "I never knew any of this." Rather than seeing a historical cover-up, she blamed herself. At New York's American Museum of Natural History, a young woman plaintively asked, "Why weren't we taught anything about this?" I heard hundreds of rhetorical or angry variations of this question.

In 1906, Booker T. Washington visited Oklahoma and was astounded by the racial mix of whites, African Americans and Native Americans. "The whole situation out here is complicated and puzzling, and if one attempts to understand it he is very deep into the intricacies of a social and political history so full of surprises that it reminds him of *Alice in Wonderland.*"

In 1986, *Black Indians* drew *Alice in Wonderland* reactions. One scholar spent a lengthy essay debating the book's title and concluded it should be *Indian Blacks.* An African American critic approvingly quoted and cited *Black Indians* over and over again and declared it "the most progressive scholarship by white people." In the age of Howard Zinn, that would amount to high praise. But in the same sentence the critic states this kind of scholarship "usually reflects . . . a white supremacist standpoint."

Odd, mixed, or confusing reactions continued. "Rudy," a young Native American friend (without African ancestry) revealed how he and his friends asked their organization to sponsor a book party for *Black Indians*, and the elders refused. He handed me documents showing that they were influenced by a

Speakers at the Schomburg Center for Research in Black History and Culture, for the 1986 book party for Black Indians

white scholar who compared my racial thinking to that of Adolf Hitler. Rudy's Native American society invited me to a meeting, and his officers asked if I was a "troublemaker." However, when invited back months later, I found a warm meeting of the minds and saw staff members of mixed descent.

Based on past experiences, Native American groups had reason to fear that the Bureau of Indian Affairs might try to use my research as an excuse to reduce allotments or other aid. But in a short while most Native Americans and societies reaffirmed their commitment to all their members.

Black Indians began with an enthusiastic book party at the Schomburg Center for Research in Black History and Culture that included eight Black Indian speakers. African American reviewers eagerly greeted the book, though some added they wanted more information than its two hundred pages provided. I was invited to share stories at Black Indian spiritual meetings in the New York area, to appear on African American and Native American media programs, and was stopped on the street by people of color who had something to say. Jim Buck, who was a Native American producer at a National Public Radio station, used the book and my contacts to develop two hour-long documentaries. And an invitation from the editor of Brooklyn's *Daily Challenge* led to my writing an unpaid op-ed column for the next twenty-two years.

Bob Law of WWRL repeatedly interviewed me on his *Night Talk* as did Imotep Gary Byrd on WLIB's the *Global Black Experience*. Gary Byrd asked me to serve as a cohost on WLIB's Columbus Day broadcasts along with Cecilia Fire Thunder of KILI, the Pine Ridge Reservation's Native American radio station. Our Columbus Day efforts raised one-fourth of KILI's annual budget.

Responses from the Black Indian community were warm and fulsome. In 1989 the National Alliance of Native Americans Longhouse made me an honorary member, and in 2000, for "fostering understanding between peoples of Native American and African Americans descent," I became the first recipient of Ohio's White Dove Peace Award. Native American and African American Studies departments on more than a few college campuses united to sponsor my presentations. And I was invited to address a protest rally in front of New York's American Museum of Natural History.

Artists unknown and well known, white and people of

color—painters, novelists, actors, writers, sculptors, and poets—responded to the book through their media. People sent along sketches, paintings, poems, books, and movie ideas. The African-Apache-Cherokee songwriting team of Lenga Tooks composed "Black Indian Woman" in its honor. In 1990, at the Brooklyn Academy of Music, Abdel Salaam staged a ballet: *Pee Dee River Bonding*, about the 1526 Black Indian colony in South Carolina, and it "had the audience cheering and leaping to its feet," noted the *New York Times* critic. I had exciting arguments and made many friends.

The Introduction to *Black Indians* expressed my hope that it would lead to "further investigation and synthesis." I never expected the startling level of scholarly reactions. In 2002, at Dartmouth College, and in 2006, at the University of Kansas, hundreds of scholars and activists assembled in national conferences to discuss what had become the new field of Black Indian studies. These intellectual exchanges produced books included in this edition's updated bibliography.

Alice Walker's towering *The Temple of My Familiar* devoted a chapter to the intrepid African and Seminole alliance that weaved its way from Florida to Oklahoma to Mexico and back to Texas. When her husband, Suwelo, gives Fanny, Walker's leading character, a copy of *Black Indians* for her birthday, she becomes enthralled with the spirited Seminoles, Wild Cat and John Horse. After she finishes the book he asks her, "What do you love about these people?," Fanny answers:

"I dunno," she said. "They open doors inside me. It's as if they're keys. To rooms inside myself. I find a door inside and it's as if I hear a humming from behind it, and then I get inside somehow, with the key the old ones give me, and are, and as I stumble about in the darkness of the room, I begin to feel the stirring in myself, the humming of the room, and my heart starts to expand with the absolute feeling of bravery, or love, or audacity, or commitment. It becomes a light, and that light enters me, by osmosis, and a part of me that was not clear before is clarified. I radiate this expanded light. Happiness."

And *that*, Suwelo knew, was called "being in love."[1]

In 1819, at the Congress of Angostura liberator, Simon Bolivar was elected president of Venezuela and planned a strategy that would free the Americas of foreign domination. He also found it necessary to clarify the racial birthright of the Americas: "The larger part of the Native population has disappeared, Europeans have mixed with the Indians and the Negroes, and Negroes have mixed with the Indians. We were all born of one mother America, though our fathers had different origins, and we all have differently colored skins. This dissimilarity is of the greatest significance."

Almost two centuries after Simon Bolivar's great truth, I am humbled by the creative use of my research and deeply moved by the love readers have shown the courageous men and women who inhabit these pages.

---

[1] Walker, Alice. *The Temple of My Familiar*. New York: Harcourt Brace Jovanovich, 1989, p. 186. Reprinted with permission.

It is a pleasure and an honor to offer this revised edition of *Black Indians*. This story is no longer hidden. I hope new readers will be as interested to meet these valiant Americans and hear their epic stories as I was to look into their lives. These men and women have earned an honored place in our history and cherished memories.

—*William Loren Katz*
June 2011

INTRODUCTION

BLACK INDIANS? THE VERY words make most people shake their heads in disbelief or smile at what appears to be a joke, a play on words. No one remembers any such person in a school text, history book, or western novel. None ever appeared.

Yet they lived and roamed all over the Americas. Their story began with the first European landings in the New World, reached from New England to Brazil, and continues today. The number of African Americans with an Indian ancestor was once estimated at about one third of the total. In Latin America the percentage is much higher. This means that an important page in history has been missing.

Three great races—red, white, and black—built the Americas together. Their contributions and their interrelationships have filled libraries with scholarly studies, history texts, and novels.

Opposite: *Diana Fletcher, Kiowa*

Black Indians of Paraguay

The relationship between Europeans and Native Americans and between Europeans and Africans have been thoroughly studied.

But one relationship has not. Conspicuous by its neglect is the relationship on this soil between red and black people. In 1920 historian Carter G. Woodson called it "one of the longest unwritten chapters in the history of the United States." He wondered if Africans did not find "among Indians one of their means to escape" from slavery.

Dr. Woodson's chapter still remains unwritten, his "escape" theory hardly explored. This book means to tackle both the chapter and the theory.

Black Indians, like other African Americans, have been treated by the writers of history as invisible. Their contributions were denied or handed to others. Where mentioned, their role has been distorted. For example, *The Negro Cowboys*, by Durham and Jones, an otherwise objective study, calls black people who joined the Indians "renegades"—a terrifying term borrowed from Hollywood westerns to describe vicious killers. *The Negro Cowboys* also declares "for every Negro renegade who joined against the white man, a company of Negro soldiers fought the Indians." This single sentence mangles some important history. It understates the number of Black Indians by hundreds of thousands. It also suggests slaves should remain loyal to their owners and praises those who "fought the Indians."

It is not that US chroniclers of the past have failed to see a Black Indian heritage through the eyes of people of color, for that is understandable. Almost all were white. What is unforgivable is that some have insisted on seeing past events through the eyes of a slaveholding and Indian-killing class that has been dead for more than a century.

But omission, not distortion, is the far more serious culprit in hiding the story of the Black Indians of the Americas. Observers, not expecting to find Africans among Indians, did not report their presence. For example, artist George Catlin painted a magnificent portrait of Chief Osceola when he and other Seminoles were held captive at Fort Multrie in 1837. Catlin never painted or mentioned that Osceola's personal bodyguard of fifty-five warriors included fifty-two Black Seminoles. Had his artistry captured their presence, he would have contributed vastly to our understanding of anthropology and history.

I have some empathy for this blindness. During research for my book, *The Black West*, I kept unearthing frontier documents and photographs that established a significant Black Indian

One Horse Charley (center) and his Shoshone friends in Reno, Nevada

presence on the US frontier. I never fully weighed my evidence and *The Black West* gave Black Indians minor attention until the third edition. As my private collection of Indian photographs and documentation piled up, it became clear the subject needed fuller treatment.

Though it is unfamiliar terrain, I have chosen to begin this story at the beginning, with the earliest foreign landings in the Western Hemisphere. This has two advantages. It establishes a Black Indian participation in democratic movements years, decades, or centuries before the American Revolution. It also demonstrates that dark people ignored the boundaries drawn by Europeans in their move from one "country" to another in search of liberty, justice, or a better life.

This unknown American story is deeply rooted in the human currents that shaped our early life. Two parallel institutions joined to create Black Indians: the seizure and mistreatment of Indians and their lands and the enslavement of Africans. In their conquest of the New World, Europeans were determined to use both dark peoples. "Ten whites are not enough to watch one Negro," said a Portuguese slave master living in Brazil in 1735. To protect slavery and prevent resistance, Europeans developed brutal methods of control and degrading racial policies.

There is evidence that European genocidal attacks on Indians in the New World may have an additional explanation besides land hunger and greed. Perhaps another reason for eliminating Indians was to prevent their alliance with Africans. Colonial Europeans left evidence aplenty that this was often an overriding fear.

RESEARCH INTO EARLY AMERICAN history confronts one with some inaccurate traditional assumptions and vocabulary. Columbus, believing he had landed in the East Indies, called the inhabitants "Indians." His error has become so much a part of our language that today even many Native Americans accept it. I have used both designations. However, I have dropped such derisive terms as *half-breed*, *renegade*, and *tribe* in characterizing Native Americans and Africans. If Europeans came from nations, so too did people of color.

I have defined Black Indians as people who have a dual ancestry or black people who have lived for some time with Native Americans. When slaves escaped to the woods and joined or began remote

Kiowa preachers of the Baptist church

communities, they are called by the Spanish term *maroons*.

In discussing the time when most foreigners in the Americas came from either Europe or Africa, I have used such words as *Spaniard* or *African*. When it is clear they were born in the Western Hemisphere, I then use such terms as *white*, *black*, or *African American*. I have not designated only US citizens as Americans for that broad category belongs to all people of the Americas. Despite their bias, I have had no choice but to accept *Latin America*, *British Colonies*, and *American Revolution* because other phrases would prove cumbersome or unclear.

I have been humbled by the awesome task of rejecting bias in so explosively controversial a topic and one peopled with so stormy a set of characters. In this story even the simple question of criminality is open to interpretation. Were those who escaped slavery seeking freedom or breaking the law? Were Black Indian maroon settlements havens of self-determination or conspiracies against the European state? One solution I have adopted has been to offer eyewitness accounts, and to see that the neglected views of Africans and Native Americans are presented.

I have never sought a bland neutrality and have consoled myself that unbiased history has yet to be written in our world. This is a labor of love that has introduced me to many exciting Americans it would have been interesting to meet. I have tried hard to balance opinions, present contrasting views, manage personal feelings, and uncover some truths.

This is a subject that deserves further investigation and synthesis. Clearly people and events described in one chapter, or even a part of one, deserve far greater study. If this effort contributes to those ends, a personal goal will have been reached.

—William Loren Katz

IF YOU KNOW I HAVE A HISTORY

TODAY MOST BLACK INDIANS do not live in the forests or on the broad plains of the United States. Most do not inhabit government reservations set aside for Native Americans any more than most Indians do. To be sure they crowd, for example, the Shinnecock reservation on New York's Long Island. But many more walk the crowded streets of nearby New York City. They are found in abundance in the cement caverns of Boston, Chicago, Denver, Cleveland, and Detroit.

They have made a long march from farms, woods, and ranches to skyscrapers, subways, and ghettoes. Most have arrived with only a faint recollection of their adventurous rural heritage and gallant ancestors. The people they meet in school, at work or play cannot appreciate their background because they know nothing about it.

"If you know I have a history, you will respect me," a Black Indian student told a conference of New York teachers in 1968. Her words still ring true. Those who assume that a people have no history worth mentioning are likely to believe they have no humanity worth defending. An historical legacy strengthens a country and its people. Denying a people's heritage questions their legitimacy.

Citizens celebrate this country's daring break from colonial rule, and rejoice in the plucky Minutemen who challenged the British at Lexington and Concord. But a month before those historic skirmishes on the path to freedom, other Americans were pursuing the same goal. Slaves in Ulster County, New York, planned a massive armed rising. Perhaps they had heard the exciting patriotic talk about liberty and independence. Their liberation plot involved slaves in Kingston, Hurley, Marbletown, and upwards of five hundred Native Americans. Unlike the Minutemen, their shot was not heard around the world, their bold conspiracy never found its way into our history books.

These dark people in Ulster County, like thousands of others mentioned in this book, made their contribution to freedom and to their immediate relatives and friends. But other Black Indians made a contribution to the entire US society that deserves consideration.

Langston Hughes, photographed in 1938, liked to trace his Native American and African ancestry.

On the snowy night of March 5, 1770, Crispus Attucks, a Black Natick Indian, stepped dramatically into US history in Boston. He was the first to fall in the Boston Massacre. Benson J. Lossing, a nineteenth-century historian, transformed Attucks into a Nantucket Indian. To Lossing it seemed wrong to place an African American with Native American blood at the daring first moment of American Independence.

Paul Cuffee, a Dartmouth Indian with African parentage, became a wealthy merchant and shipowner in early Massachusetts. He married Alice Pequit of his mother's Wampanoag Nation. But his great interest was in protecting fellow African Americans from discrimination in the United States and he became the first black man to sponsor a migration of US blacks to Africa. In 1815, he personally paid for and led thirty-eight settlers aboard his ship, *Traveller,* to Sierra Leone. Cuffe became the father of black back-to-Africa movements in this country.

Frederick Douglass, a slave runaway, with mixed African, Indian, and white ancestry, became the leading voice of black America during the Civil War era and the decades that followed. His creed, "If there is no struggle, there is no progress," has inspired reform and revolutionary movements ever since. Douglass's name and accomplishments now adorn most history texts.

Langston Hughes, poet laureate of African Americans, liked to trace his family tree back to Pocahontas. In that tree also was a man who joined John Brown's famous raid on Harper's Ferry and another who became a Virginia congressman. Hughes, a prolific writer of poetry, plays, short stories, novels, autobiographies, and newspaper columns, became the proud voice of Harlem, New York's black community.

IN THE EARLY CENTURIES of their life in the Americas, Black Indians often created a society that might have been a model for everyone. They demonstrated that there was another path through the wilderness than the one hacked out by a European lust for gold, land, and power. Their communities proved bigotry did not rise naturally from American soil, its plains and waters. Bigotry and the appetite for it were imported. They traveled the stormy Atlantic and were speedily transplanted and nourished by those who carried them over.

If they had been of a mind to, Europeans might have learned something from the dark people they selfishly used. Instead, they gathered these peoples' precious gifts and offered promises in return. Africans and Indians followed a tradition that rarely wrote matters down, but held to verbal promises. Europeans wrote many, many things down but failed to keep to their promises or treaties.

What followed in the New World was a titanic European battle for the control of dark people and natural resources. Europe marched out its best soldiers to secure a continent and subdue its people. The result was unending conquest and agonizing slavery.

But beyond the pain were armed Black Indian communities named "Hide Me" and "The Woods Lament For Me." They were home for some of our earliest explorers and pioneers. Families brought up their young, constructed homes, planted and harvested crops, took care of their elderly. They traded with neighbors, instituted religion, government, justice, and planned the common defense.

These settlements not only provided women with an equality

and respect unheard of in European society, but elevated some to leadership. Two colonial Brazilian Black Indian communities were commanded by African women, and another African maroon settlement in 1826 in Brazil was ruled by a black woman named Zeferina who successfully led her forces against towns and plantations in Bahia.

With few weapons these alliances in the woods challenged the footholds Europeans built in the Western Hemisphere. Using guerrilla tactics that would become famous in China and Vietnam in our own century, red and black people defeated superior numbers and better equipped foreign armies. This they managed while moving their families out of harm's way. These dark liberators often proved that European rule in the Americas amounted to a thin coat of white paint over a seething dark empire.

Before Patrick Henry shouted "Give me liberty or give me death!," Black Indian maroons acted on this notion. Before Thomas Jefferson wrote "all men are created equal," Black Indians turned a stirring phrase into hard reality. Before the Declaration of Independence eloquently argued for a peoples' revolution against unjust authority, thousands of dark-skinned Americans had been fighting tyrants and slavehunters on two continents.

For their audacity Black Indians faced a repression more ruthlessly cruel than any King George III imposed on the thirteen original colonies. They were forced to carry on the longest, bloodiest battle for freedom in the Western Hemisphere. Repeatedly they persuaded Europeans it was wiser to grant them independence, sovereignty, and liberty than to continue wars. European powers often learned this lesson late, after they had wasted lives and fortunes on the idea that these free colonies could be easily destroyed.

Maroon wars outlasted the endless conflicts between rival European states. Neither side gave nor asked any quarter, and prisoners were few. For their part maroons, even when captured and facing a terrible death, tried to protect their villagers. More than a century ago a British report from Belem, Brazil, described how a "captured negro gave such an account of the difficulties and dangers of the journey to his settlement, that thirty-three out of the forty [foreign] soldiers refused to accompany their captain."

To prevent Africans and Native Americans from uniting, Europeans played skillfully on racial differences and ethnic rivalries. They kept the pot of animosity boiling. Whites turned Indians into slavehunters and slaveowners, and Africans into "Indian-fighters." Light-skinned Africans were pitted against dark-skinned, free against enslaved, Black Indians against "pure" Africans or "pure" Indians.

Those who have put history into books have emphasized differences between Africans and Native Americans. For example, they have stressed that Europeans encountered Indians as distinct individuals and members of proud nations, and Africans as nameless slaves. Little mention is made of the enslavement of Native Americans and nothing is said about the cultural similarities between the two dark peoples. In 1984, scholar Theda Perdue said: "By emphasizing the actual, exaggerated and imagined differences between Africans and Indians, whites successfully masked the cultural similarities of the two races as well as their mutual exploitation by whites."

In the United States, Africans became central in the exploration of the new nation, and the development of the crucial fur trade. Because they were more able to build a binding trust among Native Americans, whites employed them as negotiators and they did not disappoint. Africans, like Native Americans, cherished their own trustworthiness and saw promises and treaties as bonds never to be broken.

In the nineteenth century a Black-Indian friendship limped on despite onslaughts from white racial policies destructive to both peoples. It survives still in the legends of Native American Nations, and in the stories and faces of many people of color.

FRONTIER MYTH AND REALITY

GENERATIONS OF YOUNG MINDS have been trained to think of life on the American frontier as a saga of white gallantry. Daring pioneers probed the wilderness. John Wayne cowboys whipped Indians to give us the USA. Children of every race rejoiced in this version of the frontier served up each Saturday afternoon at the movies.

In the real wilderness two dark people met and often united. They were not driven together by any special affinity based on a similar skin color. Their meetings were unwittingly arranged by their enemies, the Europeans, who exploited both.

But in the retelling of our western history, no one learned that Africans and Native Americans, separately and together, fought bravely for an America they knew was also theirs. Perhaps their story was trampled underfoot by their hard-riding European foes.

In 1774 patriot James Madison wrote about a slave revolt: "It is prudent such attempts should be concealed as well as suppressed." The Black Indian story has been treated as though it were a massive slave rebellion. Its final burial came at the hands of a later white generation who shaped a heritage for books and movies that ended all claims but European ones.

These frontier omissions lie at the heart of our cherished national myth. The tale of the wilderness stands as the greatest American story ever told. It is the way we wish to see ourselves. "A frontier people," said President Woodrow Wilson, "is, so far, the central and determining fact of our national history. . . . The West is the great word of our history. The Westerner has been the type and master of our American life." Creators of this west did not want it sullied by an African presence or subject to Indian claims.

"The Frontier" went from gritty reality to uplifting truth and finally to national legend. In the process entire races disappeared from view. Its cast of heroic characters included only whites. If Europeans bravely conquered continents, it was not necessary or desirable to show black and red people defying white authority to build their own communities in the wilderness. Racial stereotypes long pictured people of color as cowardly or childlike. How could red or black people be shown creating a culture in the wilderness, bravely rescuing their families, and riding off into the sunset?

There is another problem in introducing a set of dark frontier heroes. Their love of liberty thrust them against some sainted US figures. Thomas Jefferson, speaking of Indians, said "We would never stop pursuing them with war while one remained on the face of the earth." Andrew Jackson, the first great democrat to reach the White House, was first in a long line of candidates to win the presidency boasting of his Indian-fighting skills. He

Native American lacrosse players in Dallas, Texas, before World War I

waged a cruel war against Indian men, women, and children. He staunchly defended slavery and, like Jefferson, owned slaves. To save their families, Black Indians had to fight off posses and armies launched by these national heroes.

Distorting racial history, as teachers know, injures dark children. They live with a muted heritage. Despite Black Indian contributions to this land, neither black nor Indian children nor their parents have an awareness of this legacy. Like whites, Native Americans learned in school that Africans were contented slaves and had no fighting traditions, certainly none that allied them with Indians. For their part, African Americans are aware of Indians in their family trees. But they probably assume that, like the whites lurking there, they are mere intruders. Such inaccurate beliefs hide a heritage worth exploring. Further, they divide people today who could benefit from the unity forged by their ancestors.

When African Americans have pursued their genealogy, they have focused on their African roots and sought a meaningful black heritage. Children of the black awareness of the 1960s have rarely cared to mention an Indian ancestry because this might be seen as a denial of their African origins and the value of blackness. All this is part of the racial nightmare we have inherited.

With her usual perception, precision, and pride, Rosa Fay, a Black Seminole living in Brackettville, Texas, in 1943, clarified her peoples' background for pioneer researcher Kenneth W. Porter:

"We's culled people. I don't say we don't has no Injun blood, 'cause we has. But we ain't no Injuns. We's culled people."

A Navaho hunting party was photographed in the 1880s in front of their trading post.

Other Americans would benefit from a reexamination of their family trees and a new look at their biological inheritance. The process may yield wonder and gratification where once grief or skepticism ruled.

The ancestors of Black Indians often created—or died in the attempt—an American sisterhood and brotherhood we have tried to attain. They did this under terrible circumstances and in the face of armed opposition.

Had we paid proper attention to their unique model of friendship and loyalty, our common American history, from Hudson Bay to Cape Horn, might have been different, more peaceful. Our racial problems might have been more easily solved. Even at this late date we owe ourselves a rereading of this fascinating legacy. Perhaps we can still learn from and act on its lessons.

THEY FLED AMONGST THE INDIANS

ON JULY 13, 1984, the people of Roanoke Island, North Carolina, their names emblazoned on books, T-shirts, and silver commemorative medallions, began a year-long celebration. It is their proud claim that US history began with a British settlement on their island. Cultural events throughout the state announced "America's 400th Anniversary," and the US government issued a special "Roanoke Voyages" stamp.

As citizens of a relatively new nation with a short history, we leap at famous firsts and revel in antique events. People feel that our earliest ventures, properly studied, can reveal motives and character in pure form. A study of a first colony on these shores could yield insights into the nature of colonization and cast light on how and why this nation developed. Our schools spend much time studying our earliest European colonies. Teachers use this focus to teach children simple object lessons in their white ancestors' flinty determination to survive and prevail.

Bill Pickett (left) and his Black Cherokee brothers

If the children are of African or Native American descent, they learn that their ancestors lost badly and ingloriously, but that was all for the best anyway. The historical record often does not agree with these kinds of conclusions. The English newcomers sent to Roanoke Island in 1584 by Sir Walter Raleigh are a case in point. What these pioneers did was self-destruct over their own love of possession. When a silver cup allegedly disappeared, the Roanoke men roared out of their tiny enclave, muskets and torches in hand, to destroy their Indian neighbors' village and crops. This blazing display of European possession-mania cut the colony off from the one local source of help.

When the Spanish Armada severed the settlement's connection to British ports, it withered and died. Roanoke Island became famous as "the lost colony."

In light of this unacceptable object lesson for children, school texts prefer to begin US history with another colony, Captain John Smith's Jamestown, Virginia, founded in 1607. Captain Smith was sent out by a London joint-stock company seeking profits from colonization. Smith sailed with an overload of failed aristocrats and settled on land owned by the Algonquin Confederacy.

Trouble began when the newcomers refused to plant, build, or exert themselves. Iron pistol in hand, Captain Smith ordered his lazy gentlemen to "work or starve." Time and again the English were rescued from starvation through the generosity of the Algonquin Confederacy, which provided corn and bread. The foreigners responded by refusing to share their advanced agricultural tools with the Indians and violence soon broke out.

At Roanoke Island colonization proved a total failure. At Jamestown, what collapsed was the European "work ethic." No wonder some scholars decided that US history did not begin until the arrival of the hard-working Pilgrims aboard the *Mayflower* in 1620. Leaping over events can avoid some unpleasant conclusions about early European motives, character, and success.

→| |←

IF THE FIRST FOREIGN COLONY on US land is worthy of study, then another contender for this title also deserves consideration. Less than two generations after Columbus first landed in 1492, and while his son Diego served as governor of Hispaniola, an island of Spain in the Caribbean, a colony was started on the mainland of South Carolina. No one seems to want to celebrate or even mention its dramatic story and this is unfortunate. It offers a feast of insights into some errors that still cast their shadow on our racial problems.

In June 1526, Lucas Vásquez de Ayllón, a wealthy Spanish official in the city of Santo Domingo on Hispaniola, founded a colony at or near the mouth of the Pee Dee River in eastern South Carolina. Six decades before Roanoke Island, eight decades before Jamestown, and almost a century before the *Mayflower* landed at Plymouth Rock, Ayllón began his North American dream.

Ayllón's effort has been overlooked, perhaps because most people prefer to believe that US life began with the arrival of English-speaking Anglo-Saxons living under British law. Perhaps his settlement is neglected because of its tragic fate—death by mismanagement, disease, and slave revolt. Perhaps it is unmentioned because of its unique rebirth in the woods by people not considered a valued part of the US heritage.

Ayllón began preparing for his great adventure in 1520 by sending Captain Francisco Gordillo to locate a good landing site and build friendly relations with the local inhabitants. Instead, the captain teamed up with a slavehunter, Pedro de Quexos. While failing to survey a site or build good relations with anyone, the two men captured seventy Native Americans and brought them back to Santo Domingo as slaves. The first European act on what is now US soil was making slaves of free men and women.

The two adventurers returned to Ayllón with stories of naming a great river in honor of St. John the Baptist and having cut Christian crosses in trees. Ayllón was not impressed with their seizure of seventy Native Americans and brought the issue to the attention of a commission presided over by Diego Columbus. The Indians were declared free and ordered returned, but Spanish records do not show whether the order was carried out.

But they do show that Ayllón, to make amends with the natives who lost their loved ones, sent the slaver Quexos who started the problem. Once again Quexos returned with other captured natives he claimed had volunteered to serve as guides for the Spanish expedition.

Meanwhile Ayllón retained one of the original seventy, Ferdinand Chicorana, as his New World interpreter. Impressed with his skills and understanding of the mainland, he brought Chicorana to Spain to meet the king. After this meeting the king issued an order permitting Ayllón to sail for the coast of North America. The king's orders forbade enslavement of the Indians, and added "you be very careful about the treatment of the Indians." Three Dominican missionaries were sent along to protect Native Americans from the Europeans.

With this record as a backdrop, Ayllón prepared to launch his expedition to North America. After some delays his fleet of six vessels sailed from Puerto de la Plata. Aboard were five hundred Spanish men and women, one hundred enslaved Africans, six or seven dozen horses, and physicians, sailors, and the Dominican priests.

Mishap and disaster dogged the enterprise as it landed on the wrong coast, lost a ship, and Chicorana deserted. The other native interpreters seized by Quexos also fled. The Europeans were on their own.

Determined to succeed, Ayllón drove his people until they came to a great river, which was probably the Pee Dee. Selecting a location in a low, marshy area, Ayllón ordered his band to set up camp. He paused to name his settlement "San Miguel de Gualdape." When he ordered the Africans to begin building homes, he launched black slavery in the United States.

The neighboring natives fled inland and kept away. It was probably enough for them that the same Europeans who had seized seventy of their loved ones had now returned with Africans in chains.

Europeans, arriving to exploit land and labor, contrasted in many ways with the peaceful natives. The Indians lived harmoniously with nature and shared huge pine, weather-insulated homes that slept about three hundred people each. Europeans tried to construct homes that kept men and women in separate rooms. Europeans wrote that these Indians lived long lives and "their old age is robust." While European men dominated their women, Indian women doctors served their people plant juices to cure fevers.

While native life moved peacefully ahead, the foreigners slipped toward a crisis. Disease and starvation ravaged their colony and internal disputes tore it apart. The river was full of fish, but few Europeans were well enough to fish. Then an epidemic swept the settlement and before housing was in place wintery winds blew in.

Ayllón became gravely ill and died on October 18, after

having named his nephew, Johan Ramirez his successor. But Ramirez was in Puerto Rico, and the leaderless Spaniards split into bitter armed factions. Men drew swords and marched in howling winds to arrest and sometimes execute those who wished to become leaders of the colony. Some survivors complained that in the midst of their tribulations Africans began setting fires, and Native Americans sided with the slaves and made trouble.

In November a crisis erupted when Africans rebelled and fled to the Indians. One authority on slave revolts believes this was instigated by Native Americans angry over whites using their land. Africans, used to freedom in their homeland, probably needed no prodding from outside to strike for liberty. They understandably fled a dying European colony and slavery, and saw an opportunity to begin new lives in the woods among people who also hated slavery.

The surviving 150 Spanish men and women, no longer able to face a freezing winter without shelter or their labor supply, packed up and left for Santo Domingo. It would be another quarter of a century before Spaniards would again build a North American colony with slave labor.

San Miguel de Gualdape was not a total failure as the first foreign colony on US soil. The Europeans left for home after five months, but Africans remained to build their own society with the Native Americans. In the unplanned way that history meanders and careens, a new community emerged in the woods, which also included foreigners from overseas, the Africans. This new mixed settlement would soon have many American models.

In distant South Carolina forests, two and a half centuries before the Declaration of Independence, two people of color first lit the fires of freedom and exalted its principles. Though neither white, Christian, nor European, they became the first settlement of any permanence on these shores to include people from overseas. As such, they qualify as our earliest inheritance.

There is no way of knowing how long the settlement remained free of European intervention. Within a century the march of white conquest would spill into their lovely streams and forests. But while this Black Indian community lived, it provided the Americas with an example of frontier hospitality, peace, and democratic camaraderie.

Some among us will mourn the symbolic loss of the white pioneers of Roanoke Island, Jamestown, or Plymouth. The fables about them make pleasant reading. But their supporters can take heart from the brave heritage bequeathed us by the African freedom-fighters who fled San Miguel de Gualdape and by the Native Americans who took them in as sisters and brothers. Here is a gallant American tradition that ranks with those established by other fighting Americans at Concord Bridge and Valley Forge.

The story of this new community shows that our vaunted democracy did not march into the wilderness with buckled shoes and British accents. Rather it was dancing around fireplaces in South Carolina wrapped in dried animal skins and singing African and native songs before the British arrived. This dark democracy lived in family groups before London companies sent out settlers with muskets, Bibles, and concepts of private property.

The Black Indians of the Pee Dee River became the first colony on this continent to practice the belief that all people—newcomer and native—are created equal and are entitled to life, liberty, and the pursuit of happiness. Theirs is a story worth teaching our children.

IT BEGAN WITH COLUMBUS

FOR THE PEOPLE OF the Americas the arrival of Columbus was hardly a blessing. On his first day, October 12, 1492, the explorer wrote in his Diary "I took some of the natives by force." He later found the original inhabitants to be "tractable," "peaceable," and concluded "there is not in the world a better nation." His response as a European was to say that Indians must be "made to work . . . and adopt our ways."

The Christopher Columbus whose unique seamanship and courage had opened the Americas to European penetration also began the transatlantic slave trade. He started by shipping ten chained Arawak men and women to Seville, Spain. In 1498, he wrote enthusiastically to King Ferdinand and Queen Isabella about the business possibilities: "From here, in the name of the Blessed Trinity, we can send all the slaves that can be sold." When he loaded 1100 Taino men and women aboard four Spanish ships, the crowding and the stormy Atlantic crossing took a fearful toll. Only three hundred survived. But Columbus and Spain had decided to continue the profitable slave trade from the Americas. Seville became the slave capital of Spain.

Spanish priests were the first to denounce the horrors of bondage. In 1511 Dominican Friar Montesinos called slavery a mortal sin and said cruelty and tyrannny over Indians could not be justified by Christians. A few years later Bishop Las Casas, who had witnessed countless Indian massacres by his fellow

Spaniards, blamed greed for the horrors: "They kill them [Indians] because they want to be rich and have much gold, which is their sole aim." Las Casas concluded that in the New World Spaniards had become devils and Indians were the only true Christians.

Las Casas led a determined effort to halt Indian bondage. He pointed out that Indians died off by the thousands from slavery and European diseases. Forced labor in Spanish mines in the Americas was so harsh that the average worker died before he was twenty-six.

To meet their need for more laborers, Europeans looked next to Africa. The strongest sons and daughters of Africa were seized in their homes or fields or purchased from local traders. They were packed into cargo ships and shipped across the Atlantic.

Since the 1500s, this mixture of people—Native American, African American, and Spanish priests, shown here at the Shiprock Indian Agency—have been part of the southwestern US history.

Thomas Branagan, a Dublin youth who for many years served as a seaman aboard slave ships, described the boarding scene:

> Children are torn from their distracted parents; parents from their screaming children; wives from their frantic husbands; husbands from their violated wives; brothers from their loving sisters; sisters from their affectionate brothers. See them collected in flocks, and like a herd of swine, driven to the ships. They cry, they struggle, they resist; but all in vain. No eye pities, no hand helps.

The first Africans brought to the New World by European slavers probably arrived in April 1502 aboard the ship that brought the new governor of Hispaniola, Nicolas de Ovando. Soon after they landed, some Africans escaped to the woods and found a new home among the Native Americans. Later that year Governor Ovando sent a request to King Ferdinand that no more Africans be sent to the Americas. His reason was simple: "They fled amongst the Indians and taught them bad customs, and never could be captured."

Why did he feel they could never be retaken? Had the two peoples united as a military force at this early date? Were Native Americans prepared to drive off European slavehunters? Was an alliance taking shape in the woods between two peoples who opposed the Spanish conquerors? The answers to these questions are unclear.

But Governor Ovando is describing more than a problem of bad, untrustworthy servants. His words are more than a complaint about the difficulties of recapturing fugitives in a tropical rainforest. Governor Ovando's words in 1502 are the first hint of a growing problem for the European masters of the New World, the first notice of a new relationship budding beyond their control.

Africans arrived on these shores with valuable assets for both Europeans and Native Americans. They were used to agricultural labor and working in field gangs, something unfamiliar to most Indians. As experts in tropical agriculture, they had a lot to teach both white and red people. Further, Africans had a virtual immunity to European diseases such as smallpox, which wiped out Native Americans.

For Europeans seeking a source of labor that could not escape, Africans were ideal because they were three thousand miles from home. They could not flee to loved ones, as Indian slaves could. African men and women who fled could always be identified by skin color, and black became the badge of bondage.

Native Americans soon discovered that Africans had some gifts that made them uniquely valuable. Through their slave experience they qualified as experts on whites—their diplomacy, armaments, motives, strengths, and weaknesses. Escaped slaves came bearing a knowledge of their masters' languages, defenses, and plans. Sometimes Africans were able to carry off muskets, machetes, or valuable gunpowder. For these reasons their role could be crucial to Native Americans, their place secure in village life. A common foe, not any special affinity of skin color, became the first link of friendship, the earliest motivation for alliance.

Next the two peoples began to discover they shared some vital views of life. Family was of basic importance to both, with children and the elderly treasured. Religion was a daily part of cultural life, not merely practiced on Sundays. Both Africans and Native Americans found they shared a belief in economic cooperation rather than competition and rivalry. Each people was proud, but neither was weighed down by prejudice. Skill, friendship, and trust, not skin color or race were important. Since Indians willingly adopted people into their villages, Africans found they were welcome.

In the century following Columbus's landing, millions of Native Americans died from a combination of European diseases, harsh treatment, and murder. Africans took their places in the mines and fields of the New World. The estimated 80 million Native Americans alive in 1492 became only 10 million left alive a century later. But the 10,000 Africans working in the Americas in 1527, had by the end of the century become 90,000 people.

These figures are even more striking within local areas. In 1519 when the Spaniards arrived, Mexico had a population of 25 million Indians. By the end of the century only a million were still alive. The invader calculated that more profit would be made if laborers were worked to death and replaced. In their plans pain and suffering did not count, and no cruelty was considered excessive.

Out of the shifting labor forces a new population emerged of mixed Africans and Native Americans. By 1650 Mexico alone had an African-Indian population (some with white ancestry) of one hundred thousand. A new race was being born.

In 1510 King Ferdinand, visions of gold dancing before his eyes, lifted all restrictions on sending Africans to the Americas. He promised to send all that were needed and include "a trustworthy person" to be in charge of each group. In this way,

When captured, Native American resistance leaders were ceremonially put to death. In 1512, Hatuey, a Taino who fought the invaders in Hispaniola and Cuba, was captured and was asked him by a priest if he first wanted to accept Baptism so he could enter heaven and meet God. No, he answered, I would only find more Christians there.

Caribe Indians were among the earliest victims of Spain's invasion.

he said, slaves and masters would "share in the gold they may collect" and slaves would receive "ease if they work well." This was an idle dream.

The slave population expanded, but was never rewarded with ease for its great toil. European masters continued to drive those in chains as hard as they could. Ease only came when people escaped to the forests and swamps. Increasingly Africans and the remaining enslaved Indians fled their masters and created their own secret colonies beyond European eyes. In time these would pose the most disruptive challenge the European colonial system faced in the Americas.

In the age of Columbus and Las Casas this threat was not clear. Europeans counted their profits and kept importing Africans. In 1511 Governor Ovando forgot his opposition to importing Africans as slaves. "One black," he marveled, "can do the work of four Indians." Here, he believed, was a danger worth the price. His fellow Europeans heartily agreed with him. From then on slavery would expand, brutality would keep it in place, and whites would reap enormous profits.

3
BETWEEN THE RACES WE CANNOT DIG TOO DEEP A GULF

IN 1522 EUROPEANS IN the Americas first learned that slavery did not easily or painlessly lead to enormous wealth. On Christmas Day, African and Indian slaves on a plantation owned by Diego Columbus rose and murdered their masters and overseers. Nearby Native Americans joined the rebels. The beautiful island of Hispaniola shook with one of the first recorded slave rebellion in the New World.

The conspiracy had spread across the sprawling sugar plantations in the weeks before Christmas. Patiently the plotters waited until Christmas Day when the planters and their families would be bloated with food, soaked with liquor, and too weak or sleepy to offer much resistance. Then they struck, plunging into the night to kill whites and find freedom.

For two days they met little opposition, but on the third Spanish troops caught up with the rebels in an open field and opened fire. The fugitives broke for the woods. The Europeans were unfamiliar with the treacherous terrain near the city of

Santo Domingo. Few were willing to pursue their most dangerous slaves into an area suited to guerrilla warfare.

Governor Diego Columbus, his Spanish troops and advisors, decided on a new strategy. The governor hired Native Americans for the dangerous task of tracking the fugitives. A hunt began. The exact outcome is unclear.

SLAVERY AND RESISTANCE SPREAD

MASTERS AND SLAVES LEARNED some important lessons from this first bloody confrontation. Enslaving Indians and Africans was not going to be free of pain. Masters in a slave land would not sleep easily each night. Europeans concluded it was absolutely necessary to remain armed, and use one race to fight the other. A French colonial dispatch later in the century put the matter simply: "The law is hard, but it is both wise and necessary in a land of 15 slaves to one white. Between the races we cannot dig too deep a gulf."

The enslaved also learned some lessons. Their owners would rise to any level of violence and arm anyone to protect bondage and their grip on the Americas. Europeans would throw their own soldiers into the fray or hire Indians living nearby. Slaves began to reason that their success might depend upon their ability to make friends among neighboring Indians. Friends do not hunt friends.

The European policy of divide and conquer that began on Christmas Day, 1522, introduced elements of deep division to the Americas. Slavery and its cruel legacy left a bloody trail across the grass and soil of the Americas. It spread southward and westward from the Caribbean to Mexico and along the coastline of South America to Cape Horn where Atlantic and Pacific oceans meet.

But another American tradition also took root. The men and women enslaved in the New World began a pattern of resistance. The first enslaved were the first to flee, the first to rebel, the first to announce that chains were meant to be broken.

The spirit of rebellion spread like a wildfire that no European power could put out. In the next ten years revolts spread to Colombia, Panama, Cuba, Puerto Rico, and Mexico. In 1537 a major insurrection threatened Spanish headquarters at Mexico City. Viceroy Antonio de Mendoza reported that Africans "had chosen a King, and had agreed . . . to kill all the Spaniards . . . and that the Indians were also with them." Terrified Mexican officials agreed to halt any further importations of Africans. Slave resistance had temporarily halted the African slave trade.

By the 1570s the flames of revolt were burning brightly in Mexico. One in every ten slaves was living a free life in hiding. Alarmed about the safety of whites, Viceroy Martin Enriquez (1568–1580) wrote to the king of Spain:

> Your Majesty, . . . the time is coming when these [African] people will have become masters of the Indians, inasmuch as they were born among them and their maidens, and are men who dare to die as well as any Spaniard in the world. . . . I do not know who will be in a position to resist them.

It was in Mexico that Europeans tested their strongest effort to keep Africans apart from Native Americans. Black men far outnumbered their women and so sought Indian wives. A Native American wife meant, if she was free, that children born to her would be free, not slaves. So extensive was the contact between red and black people that Spanish law prohibited the two races from living together or marrying. As early as 1523, Hernando Cortés was given a Royal Order to keep Indians in their villages, apart from Africans at all costs. (This was only seven years after Venice, Italy, isolated its Jews in the first ghetto in history.)

One Royal Order forbade "trade, commerce or communication" between the two peoples of color. They were forbidden to sell chickens, fruit, and vegetables, and both defied the law.

This early French engraving of the Osage Indian Nation captures many skin colors, though the artist has given all a "Roman" nose.

Racial mixing was so common in Mexico that it became hard to tell by skin color who was free and who was slave. King Philip complained that young Black Indians committed crimes and then dressed as Indians so they could "hide out with their mother's relatives and cannot be found." The genetic blending of the two peoples clearly weakened the control Europeans wanted over their slaves. Europeans feared any dark person might be a slave driven to desperation or out for revenge. "One lived in constant fear," wrote a Spanish colonist.

MAROON SETTLEMENTS

FROM THE TIME OF Columbus the gravest threat to European domination of the Western Hemisphere came from outlaw communities of former slaves. These maroon colonies, as they were called, were considered a knife poised at the throat of the slave system. Some fearful Europeans saw them as a sword pressed against the entire colonial system in the Americas, and they had a point.

Men and women maroons saw their settlements as the fulfillment of an American dream—a sheltered home in freedom. They were a place for families to educate their young, develop their agriculture and trade, practice religion, justice, and government. As outlaw communities they operated in remote, difficult-to-find and hard-to-defeat locations. Maroons considered each day of survival a small miracle, and were thankful for each new dawn as free men and women.

Some colonies were begun by a single African or Indian, and others were the result of several or many slaves fleeing together. The history of the Saramaka people of Surinam in South America started around 1685 when African and native slaves escaped and together formed a maroon society. For eight generations Dutch armed forces tried to crush their community, but today it is still alive and boasts twenty thousand members. For the Saramakans liberty came in 1761 when Europeans abandoned their wars and sued for peace.

From their first day maroon colonies faced enormous problems. They had to quickly find a safe location, plan a defense, feed and clothe their people, and plan the life of a stable community. Women were usually in short supply, and many maroon raids sought to bring back African or Indian wives. Families

This early French print, America, *shows Native Americans and Africans dancing together, a universal symbol of friendship.*

meant that communities would last, remain at peace, and that their soldiers would fight harder for their loved ones and children were at risk.

Some maroons perched near large cities and lived as bandits. They raided local plantations, merchants, and even Indians and slaves. Their communities were unstable, often had few women and children, and usually disappeared into the violence they helped create. Although some earned a reputation for daring raids on rich Europeans, many were feared by people of every race.

Fear of attack haunted every maroon settlement. It was a danger they could count on. Johannes King, an African who lived among the Matawai Indians in the Guianas in 1885, recalled his peoples' struggle to stay alive during decades of warfare.

> Here is the story of our ancestors and of their difficulties while they were at war with the bakra [whites]. At that time they suffered severe shortages and were living under dreadful conditions, but the lack of food was their worst problem. They didn't even have time to clear and plant gardens to produce food. The whites were always pursuing and attacking. . . . They slashed the crops to bits, ruining everything they saw. They set fire to everything they didn't want to carry off with them. Well, that enraged our early ancestors against the whites.

The planning of defense and agriculture in most Black Indian settlements drew largely on African models and experience. However, no type of influence was discarded. These colonies grasped aspects of Indian, African, and even slave life considered vital for survival.

The African influence was strongest in tropical maroon locations, and there African methods of planting, irrigation, and harvesting held sway under African-type governments. Africans, as experts on tropical agriculture, had a lot to teach both Indians and Europeans. A leading defense technique—planting sharp sticks in a pit and covering it with thick grass to trap intruding armies—was African. It not only inflicted terrible damage, but terrified any invading army with the thought that a sudden, horrible death could occur at any moment. These pits were almost impossible to detect.

Men and women, who once were starved and beaten by masters, grew strong and vigorous in these hidden communities. Maroon settlements took such daring names as: God Knows Me and None Else, Disturb Me If You Dare, Come Try Me If You Be Men, and I Shall Moulder Before I Shall Be Taken.

Maroon self-esteem seemed to grow with each month of liberty. It also sprang from the knowledge that Europeans were often afraid to march out and challenge their communities' defenses. "Their self-respect grows because of the fear whites have of them," wrote a Portuguese colonist to King João in 1719.

Maroon music also reflected the confidence settlements had in their military strength. A maroon song, preserved for generations in Brazil, assured villagers their enemies were doomed:

> Black man rejoice
> White man won't come here
> And if he does,
> The Devil will take him off.

Maroon culture drew from the experiences of Africa's nations, Native Americans, and what people of color learned about Europeans as slaves or free men and women. Africans, so far from home, made special efforts to preserve their ancestral ways and pass them on to their children and others who would listen. African patterns, prominent in farming and defense, were also important in government, administration of justice, and religion.

Many maroon colonies adopted forms of Christianity, but allowed a number of competing religions to flourish. In some villages and families mystic religions played a vital part in the way people faced the threats around them. Maroons felt convinced each day still alive was worthy of a blessing to a powerful outside force.

To the surprise of Europeans, many maroon colonies became successful, independent farming communities. In the eighteenth century Captain John Stedman, leading Dutch troops against maroons in the Guianas, wrote that maroon foods were superior to European products and in great supply. Men and women in maroon settlements were often described as healthy, tall, and muscular, a tribute to their diets and to their freedom.

For some colonies trade became a vital part of economic life. Men and women ventured out to exchange their farm produce for valuable guns and ammunition, and sometimes gold and jewelry. Trade was carried on with slaves and masters, Indians and Europeans, and free black people.

The prosperity of some colonies made them an object of envy and then attack by Europeans. Those maroons most likely to face military assaults by invading armies were situated on land Europeans wanted. Others were invaded because they

Maroon leaders are sentenced by a French colonial court.

were engaged in businesses whites sought to control.

Black Indians in Venezuela in 1728, for example, ran a successful shipping operation Europeans wanted. Led by a man named Juan Andresote, they carried cacao from Spanish merchants in the Yaracuy valley to Dutch merchants on Curaçao about 150 miles away. Philip V of Spain awarded his European friends a monopoly of this trade, placing them on a collision course with the business run by Andresote. In 1732 Spain sent out 250 soldiers, including 150 men conscripted from Indians and African slaves, to challenge the businessmen of Andresote.

Outside the town of Cabria, Andresote quickly changed from shipping expert to guerrilla warrior. He maneuvered his army into battle with such skill that the slave and native soldiers deserted the European command. Andresote's sharpshooters' musket fire then brought down all but forty-four European soldiers.

But Spain had not given up. It sent 1500 troops after Andresote, and he had to slip off to Curaçao to save his life. His brother, José Francisco, rallied the Black Indians, but they were no match for such an overwhelming force. However, it did take Spain another five years to eliminate their dark business competitors in the Yaracuy valley.

It is unclear whether Europeans more often fought or traded with their Black Indian competitors. Colonial law often threw whites into jail for trading with the outlawed maroon communities on their borders. But some Europeans considered this a cost to be borne in carrying on a successful business. It may have seemed strange to have former slaves and their former masters trading like equals, but both saw a profit in the exchange and conducted themselves like good business people.

MAROON GOVERNMENTS AND LEADERS

MAROON SETTLEMENTS WERE AN effort to re-create a free society by people who had once lived free. Before 1700 most maroon leaders were—like their followers—African-born. Some of these colonies built dynasties on African models that lasted for generations and had royal courts, cabinets, princes, and princesses.

By the beginning of the eighteenth century maroon figures were cut from a different mold. They were born in the Americas, often of Black Indian stock. Their skills were in dealing with Europeans in battle and at the negotiating table. They preferred to be known as governor or commander rather than king or queen. Most leaders still had a familiarity with African traditions and customs.

Women played a crucial role in maroon life and were considered for leadership. Filippa Maria Aranha, an African, ruled a thriving colony in Amazonia, Brazil. Her daring forays against the Portuguese armies sent against her village not only defeated them, but convinced the enemy it was wiser to negotiate than try to defeat her. At the bargaining table Aranha won her people's liberty and sovereignty. In Passanha, Brazil, the Portuguese discovered Malali Indians and Africans living under the rule of another African woman.

Leading a maroon colony took a rare combination of wisdom, toughness, and skill. The ruler had to provide for a strong defense, keep spirits high despite threats, and develop a rich and satisfying economic life for members. Courts or other means of administering justice had to be in place and considered fair. Because of the threat from outside, enforcement of rules was often harsh and swift. On vital matters such as murder, robbery, adultery, or desertion, the punishment was death, often in public.

A Dutch artist sketched this armed maroon figure.

Since women were outnumbered by men in maroon settlements, women were not only protected, but sometimes permitted to have more than one husband. This arrangement was carried out under careful rules that kept jealousy from disrupting village life. In this as in all other matters preserving unity and providing a strong defense came first. These settlements also protected the young and the elderly with special care, since the former represented the future and the latter represented gallant traditions and valuable knowledge.

Maroon leaders were first and foremost military figures. For over four centuries in Latin America European armed forces waged a war to the death against them.

Captain John Stedman, a British officer in charge of Dutch troops in Guiana at the time of the American Revolution, left a record of his maroon campaigns. He told how his troops, which included Europeans and Indians, destroyed "the most beautiful field of ripe rice" and left a village of one hundred homes "in smoking ruins." Captain Stedman, his eighty marines and twenty rangers, enjoyed their devastation, and he proudly wrote of "the continued noise of the firing, shouting and swearing, and hallooing of black and white men mixed together; the groans of the wounded and dying, all weltering in blood and dust."

To delay or defeat these well-armed soldiers, maroons had to devise careful and unique strategies. In one battle Stedman's men all suffered wounds from maroon musket fire, but realized they had only minor injuries. Instead of bullets embedded in their flesh, they found pebbles, coat buttons, and pieces of silver coins. These maroons had no bullets.

On the night after the battle, Stedman's troops found

themselves in the midst of a shouting match with their maroon foes. All night voices from the woods hurled curses and ridicule at the invaders, and the Europeans shouted back their fury at being kept awake. The next morning Stedman's soldiers discovered that, under the cover of that noise, the maroons had moved out their women, children, and elderly, their rice, yams, and other possessions. The Captain thought this tactic "would have done honor to any European commander."

By the time Captain Stedman and his soldiers left for Holland in 1776, the maroon forces had grown from three thousand to fifteen thousand. Sixty years later they were seventy thousand strong and enjoying their liberty, prosperity, and independence.

To defeat them, Captain Stedman had relied on conscripted Indian and slave soldiers. This became a common European practice. These troops proved to be the best jungle fighters the Europeans had. They also were the least reliable, the most likely to defect to the people they were sent off to destroy. European soldiers and officers rarely relished marching into the wilderness to face seasoned jungle fighters, so they continued to conscript, bribe, or hire Native Americans and Africans.

THE REPUBLIC OF PALMARES

FOR ALMOST A CENTURY a maroon colony called the Republic of Palmares, in northeastern Brazil, stood as the greatest challenge to European rule in Latin America. It began around 1600 with a few African slave runaways and friendly Indians. In 1640 a Dutch citizen named Lintz reported eleven thousand people living in Palmares's three villages. The Dutch West India Company decided to put Palmares through "fire and sword." They tried again a few years later, also without success.

By then Palmares was half a mile long, with streets six feet wide, and had hundreds of homes, churches, and shops. Its well-kept lands produced cereals and other crops irrigated African-style with streams. It boasted courts that carried out justice for its thousands of citizens, and was ruled over by King Ganga-Zumba. (Ganga-Zumba combined an Angolan African word for *great* with a Tupi Indian word for *ruler*.) Christianity was commonly practiced, including elaborate marriage and baptism ceremonies that drew large crowds.

In 1657, life in Palmares was still relatively peaceful. But the new rulers of Brazil, the Portuguese, decided it must be destroyed. A foreign expedition was launched about every fifteen months to obliterate the Republic of Palmares, and each was beaten back with heavy losses on both sides. Palmares, its determined armed forces, and three huge surrounding walls, cost many a foreign commander or governor his post or his life. Men in splendid uniforms turned and fled back to Rio de Janeiro or Lisbon, relieved to abandon a war they could not win.

A seventeenth-century Portuguese soldier wrote of these failures: "The army's best fighters, the most experienced leaders ... were at once employed for this purpose, with immense effort and suffering, but very little was achieved."

Finally, in 1694, the invaders brought in an army of Brazilian Indians called "Paulistas" to lead the massive assault on the Republic of Palmares. Some six thousand Paulistas, supported by Portuguese soldiers and weapons, laid seige to Palmares for

After almost a century of freedom, the Republic of Palmares was overthrown in 1694 by Portuguese forces and their Native American allies.

forty-two days. On February 5 it was overrun, with hundreds dying in hand-to-hand combat. Other hundreds, including Palmares's bravest warriors, according to a legend, hurled themselves over a cliff rather than surrender.

The ruler, King Zambi, who had been wounded in the struggle, was captured and beheaded by the enemy. His head was displayed, said the European victors, "to kill the legend of his immortality."

But death does not kill legends. For almost a century the Republic of Palmares had shone as the brightest star of freedom in Latin America. It had united many peoples under an African form of government and culture. For generations it had turned around European invaders and their hired mercenaries. Each time it had returned to planting and harvesting abundant crops.

The meaning of Palmares and its legendary rulers was that people of color in the Western Hemisphere meant to be free. This idea terrified Europeans more than the powerful armies and defenses of Palmares.

THE PRESIDENT OF MEXICO

IN 1615 KING PHILIP II of Spain received a letter from his Mexican colony advising him that "division of the races is an indispensable element" in controlling his colonies. But people of color had also learned the reverse was true, that their best road to success in resisting foreign domination was to unite. This became clear during the crucial war for independence Mexico fought against Spain early in the nineteenth century.

Not only did Mexico's maroon experience prepare its mixed races to march to independence, but it cast up a leader in Vincente Guerrero, a Black Indian. Born in Ixtla in 1782, Guerrero's parents were of mixed European, Indian, and African stock. As a young man, Guerrero became a mule driver, and in 1810, he was one of the first to enlist in the war for independence.

In his first battle, he was commissioned a captain. As the conflict dragged on for years, the leading revolutionaries died or were captured. But with two thousand ragged men carrying guns and ammunition taken from fallen Spanish soldiers, Guerrero kept the spark of rebellion alive in the Sierra

President Vicente Guerrero of Mexico

Madre mountains. Repeatedly Spanish officials tried to persuade the charismatic young man to surrender and return home. They even sent his father to ask him to accept a pardon. Guerrero fought on.

By 1821 the independence movement was headed toward success. Guerrero's incorruptibility gave it strength and drew peasant support. "His swarthy face, resonant voice, and flashing eyes made him an object of profound respect even among his enemies," reported US historian H. H. Bancroft. In 1824 Guerrero, who had only learned to read a few years before (when he was forty), helped shape the Mexican Constitution. He wrote the provision "All inhabitants whether White, African, or Indian, are qualified to hold office."

In 1829 the former mule driver became president of Mexico. He began a program of far-reaching reforms, abolishing the death penalty, starting construction of schools and libraries for the poor. He ended slavery in Mexico. Yet, because of his skin color, lack of education, and country manner, he was held in contempt by the upper classes in Mexico City.

This president who had, according to Bancroft, "a gentle-ness and magnetism that inspired love among his adherents," was still "a triple-blooded outsider."

Black historian J. A. Rogers summarized Guerrero's striking accomplishments by calling him "the George Washington and Abraham Lincoln of Mexico."

THE FINEST-LOOKING PEOPLE I HAVE EVER SEEN

FIRST THEY CAME ONE or two at a time, strong young men and women beating a path from slavery into the thickets and marshes of Florida. Soon others joined them, sisters and brothers, mothers and fathers, then the elderly and the very young. Parents carried babies or children, some injured during escape. Daring men returned to Georgia

Using muskets seized from their foes, Seminole men fought for the right to live free in Florida.

and Alabama to fetch mothers, fathers, wives, children, and friends who needed help in reaching freedom.

Florida proved unique in US history—a location where large communities of ex-slaves could live hidden from enemy eyes. Escaped slaves living as maroons became Florida's first settlers. Dense jungles, high grass, deadly reptiles, alligators, hordes of insects, and tropical diseases waited for all who entered.

These conditions also protected Africans from European invading forces. Historian Joseph Opala has written: "Politically, Florida was in the hands of its new inhabitants. That it was colored Spanish on the map was largely for the amusement of white men."

Generations before Thomas Jefferson sat down to write the Declaration of Independence. Florida's dark runaways wrote their own. It used no paper or ink and was constructed of spears, arrows, and captured muskets. But it issued a warning of "keep out!" and "leave us alone, or else die." It said "liberty or death."

SEMINOLES AND AFRICANS

AROUND THE TIME AFRICAN settlers arrived in Florida, refugees fleeing the Creek Nation also settled there. This group called themselves "Seminoles" or runaways, and their Muskogee culture accepted a variety of Indian ethnic groups—Yuchi, Hitchiti, and Alabama. For Seminole people used to admitting those who were different, it was easy to accept Africans.

Africans proved far more familiar with Florida's tropical terrain than Spaniards or Seminoles. They transplanted a rice cultivation method practiced in Senegambia and Sierra Leone.

Used to a more moderate climate, Seminoles began to learn how to survive in Florida from these ex-slaves. "From the beginning of Seminole colonization in Florida," writes Opala, "the Indian may have depended upon African farmers for their survival."

The Seminole Nation offered their new friends some valuable gifts in return. Africans and other ethnic groups enjoyed an independent village status. Their only obligation was to pay a small agricultural tax to be used for the common defense.

If Africans needed something besides freedom, it was a strong defense against slavehunters from the north, so their tax was well spent. Georgia slaveholders were soon invading Florida, seeking their runaways, and were soon meeting a united resistance by red and black armed forces.

Black Seminoles tried to live a peaceful life in their towns and around their ceremonial plazas ruled by their own chiefs. While they were shaping a sturdy agricultural community, British officers to the north provided weapons and military advisors for desperadoes ready to raid Florida for slave fugitives.

With hostile British forces closing in on its Florida border as early as 1587, Spain recruited anyone willing to fight these invaders. Florida became a Spanish buffer zone protected by Native American and African warriors, assisted by a sprinkling of pirates, smugglers, and others.

In 1739 slave fugitives living in St. Augustine built a fort to protect their families and stem British incursions. Spain, with few of its own soldiers, was pleased to have their lands protected by these dark men. The English were furious about a fort guarded by hundreds of armed Africans and their Indian allies.

Black Seminoles played a vital part in the coalition against the slave power to the north. Their knowledge of farming in

Florida was second to none. They also brought the kind of information slaves always have about their masters' ways of thinking. One observer described them as "stout and even gigantic . . . the finest looking people I have ever seen." They seemed immune to the malaria and small pox that devastated Indians and Europeans.

British and then US slaveholders were horrified by the strong relationships among red and black Seminoles. Each owed the other a measure of devotion and service, and this was hardly what whites had come to expect from Africans. Black Seminoles had well-built homes and raised fine crops of corn, sweet potatoes, vegetables, and cotton. They owned herds of livestock and had time for hunting and fishing. They were known for their excellent fighting skills, a major in the Georgia militia calling them the Seminoles' "best soldiers."

By the nineteenth century Black Seminoles had become key advisors and valuable interpreters for the nation. They were familiar with English, Spanish, and the Muskogee or Hitchiti Seminole languages. Not all African runaways from slavery lived among the Seminoles for some had formed their own maroon settlements. Against slaveholders, however, all united.

THE FIRST SEMINOLE WAR

GEORGIA SLAVEHOLDERS SOON UNDERSTOOD that Black Seminole camps could put an end to their slave system. To extinguish this beacon attracting the daring among their slaves, a group calling themselves "Patriots" plotted to annex Florida.

After the destruction of Fort Negro in 1816, US forces and Creek mercenaries lead prisoners back to slavery in Georgia.

Acting on information that a massive assault was being planned, Seminoles struck first at US plantations. When St. Augustine blacks joined the attack, desertions from plantations began to swell Seminole ranks. With surprise raids Seminoles destroyed a US wagon train, bottled up the Georgia militia, and assassinated the Patriot leader.

President James Madison, who had been giving the Patriot cause covert support, had to withdraw his aid.

But the US slaveholder presence began to undermine the equality between red and black Seminoles. Blacks, though still teachers and advisors, now desperately needed Seminole protection against US slavehunters. The United States, the giant to the north, threatened Seminole land and peace. But for Black Seminole families, liberty itself was at stake.

The United States, represented by General Andrew Jackson, hero of New Orleans, prepared to wipe out Seminole resistance. Black Seminoles had taken over a British fortress supplied with four cannons, sitting on the Apalachicola River on the Florida panhandle. "Fort Negro" was largely manned by black officers and men under the direction of Commander Garcia.

Garcia, a lean, tense, tight-lipped man was known for his cunning, courage, and cruelty. He was well-suited to his moment in history. His forces included three hundred Seminole men, women, and children, most of whom were either black or mixed; only thirty-four were pure red Seminoles. Garcia hoped his fortress and troops would shield the Seminole plantations that lined the riverbanks for fifty miles. There peaceful men and women raised crops, tended cattle, and brought up children.

It was clear it would take a miracle to dislodge Garcia and his followers from behind their three-walled fortress. It was situated in a treacherous swamp area impossible to storm. Each month more slaves joined Garcia's band, and to add to his numbers, Garcia's soldiers ventured outside to raid plantations.

Under General Jackson's orders and without a declaration of war, General Gaines marched a massive force of regular US troops, Marines, and five hundred Creek Indian mercenaries. His mission as spelled out by General Jackson was to blow up Fort Negro and "restore the stolen negroes . . . to their rightful owners." The invaders were aided by US Navy ships.

On a hot day in late July 1816, US armed forces and Creeks under Chief McIntosh stood before Fort Negro and demanded its surrender. Garcia's men raised a British flag, and just to antagonize their adversaries, a bloody red flag that dared them to fight. A delegation of Creek leaders sent to receive Garcia's surrender were punched, insulted, and sent back. To make his point Garcia fired off a cannon shot.

A young surgeon with the infantry that day, Marcus Buck, reported, "We were pleased with their spirited opposition, though they were Indians, negroes and our enemies." It was soon clear, wrote Buck, "most of them determined never to be taken alive."

Each side fired off cannonballs that landed harmlessly in the mud or shallow water. Eight times US ships fired and eight times no one inside Fort Negro was hit. A ninth cannonball, heated red hot in a ship's furnace, landed with miraculous accuracy inside the fort's ammunition dump. In an instant Fort Negro was a roar of flames as hundreds of barrels of gunpowder exploded.

In the smoking ruins the US invaders found 270 dead, three uninjured and sixty-four wounded, some fatally. Garcia, found alive, was executed and the surviving men, women, and children marched back to slavery in Georgia.

The US public heard nothing about this massacre for twenty years. In 1837 New York Judge William Jay broke the story.

The quick US victory on the Apalachicola proved to be the beginning, not the end of Seminole resistance, the first of three Seminole wars that lasted for decades. Even as the invaders rejoiced in a lucky cannon shot, hundreds of Seminole families hurried southeast to join Chief Billy Bowlegs on the Suwannee River.

There they built new homes all the way to Tampa Bay and resumed life as farmers and fishermen, cattle herders and horse breeders. By early 1817 some five hundred red and black Seminoles were drilling, parading to the beat of drums, and preparing for the next battle.

Meanwhile General Andrew Jackson and the James Madison

In 1824 this Seminole delegation to Washington relied on the interpreter, Negro Abraham (center, back).

Administration made plans for Florida. General Gaines moved his troops out to burn down the Black Seminole village of Fowltown. Believing it was best for citizens to learn little of the mounting US war in Florida, the US secretary of war kept Congress in the dark.

By the time President James Monroe took office in 1817, Jackson proposed a secret plan. "Let it be signified to me through any channel that the possession of the Floridas would be desirable to the United States and in sixty days it will be accomplished." Jackson waited patiently for his signal.

In January 1818, Jackson, with two mounted regiments and a fleet at his command, marched on Billy Bowlegs's towns, "search and destroy" fashion. By May 24, Jackson captured

This 1790s engraving shows slavehunters pursuing runaways into swamps.

Pensacola, and without a declaration of war, Florida passed into US hands.

Congress greeted Jackson's brash illegality with a mixture of criticism and praise. In 1819 the United States paid Spain $5 million for Florida, making Jackson's seizure appear to be a real estate purchase.

From the beginning of its interest in Florida, the United States was astounded and infuriated by the easy mixture of races in the Seminole Nation. It constantly sought to divide the two peoples. General Gaines told Seminole King Hatchy, "You harbor a great many of my black people among you at the Suwannee," and asked "to go by you against them." Gaines even promised, "I will not hurt anything belonging to you."

King Hatchy was also definite: "I harbor no negroes. . . . I shall use force to stop any armed Americans from passing my towns or on my lands." Neither side would budge.

For years, the United States sent its enormous resources of troops, ships, and military supplies to crush Seminole resistance to its slaveholding way of life. Since it was clear the giant to the north would never accept an independent, armed, and confident free black community inside a slaveholding nation, Seminoles braced for war.

Jackson's invasion of 1818 did more than take Florida from Spain. It threw the United States into a war to prevent the Black Seminole alliance from disturbing the South's plantation system. Slaveholder James Monroe secretly ordered the invasion, and slaveholder General Andrew Jackson conducted it to provide the president "plausible deniability." Secretary of State John Quincy Adams lied to Congress about the war's intent, massacres, and clear violation of the Constitution. Only Congress can declare war. Adams further declared opponents of the war were "aiding the enemy" and said Jackson's atrocities were efforts at "peace, friendship and liberality."

To these leaders Florida's African Seminole alliance was a dangerous beacon light, refuge, and massive underground railroad for their slaves, writes historian William Weeks. They feared it would trigger a rebellion that could destroy the US plantation system. Their words and actions as government officials, Weeks writes, remind "historians not to search for truth in the official explanation of events."

First the US Army drove the Black Seminoles into southern Florida. By 1823, Seminoles had agreed to live on reservations. In 1826, Seminole King Philip (or Emathla) protested: "Here our navel strings were first cut and the blood from them sunk into the earth and made the country dear to us."

To disrupt their racial alliance, US officials promoted slavery among the Seminoles. Of the Five Nations, only the Seminoles rejected the kind of slavery the United States wanted. Wealthy Creeks, who owed their riches to slave labor, were sent to persuade Seminole chiefs to become slave masters. Whites and Creek Indians were encouraged to raid Seminole villages for slaves. Free Seminole men, women, and children were carried off and sold in southern slave markets.

The position of Black Seminoles, once secure within the nation, now needed strong support from Seminole leaders. Division entered villages as chiefs argued various courses of action that might leave them in peace. Some Seminoles claimed they now "owned" their black members, since that was the only language whites understood. But some who claimed this ownership took advantage of it and sent their black villagers off to hard labor in their fields.

Seminole law making it impossible to sell a slave remained firmly in place. Seminole leaders still married black women and had black military and diplomatic advisors. But US policy had begun to erode a strong friendship and trust and to bend equality.

In the face of their changing relations some Black Seminoles left to form their own settlements, and in 1822 the US secretary of state reported that in Florida there were "five or six hundred maroon negroes wild in the woods." Further south on the peninsula there were even more. Florida now had a growing number of maroons who owed allegiance only to themselves.

For US slaveholders, the armed, independent Black Seminoles were an intolerable problem. They owned horses, cattle, hogs, and chickens and tended their own gardens. Worse, they were treated as kindly as family members—which they often were. In 1835 US Indian Agent Wiley Thompson reported they had "equal liberty with their owners." They carried guns, were allowed to travel long distances, and acted "impudently" free.

These were not slaves, complained US masters, but people

General Andrew Jackson used savage dogs in his war against the African-Seminole alliance in Florida, as shown in this 1830 artist's sketch.

who kept their African names, dressed in fine Seminole clothing and turbans, adopted Seminole stomp dances, sang Seminole and African songs.

In this leniency, slave masters saw a grave threat to their nearby slave system. Seminole seeds of revolution might overtake their own plantations and bloody the countryside with racial outbreaks. Florida would not be a fit place for slavery until the Seminole Nation behaved like proper slaveowners.

THE SECOND SEMINOLE WAR

IN 1835 WARFARE ERUPTED again between US troops and Seminoles. One alleged cause was the seizure by a US officer of Chief Osceola's black wife. Even if this story is more myth than truth, it symbolizes a unity of two races under Osceola's command.

A more basic cause of hostilities was the continued US use of tricks and force to have Seminole chiefs sign treaties agreeing to leave Florida for reservation land in Arkansas and Oklahoma. When Seminole leaders were tricked into signing a treaty, hostilities broke out.

Most alarmed were Black Seminoles. They reasoned that under any US agreement, they would be forced into bondage. In December 1835, King Philip led black and red Seminoles in a raid on a US plantation. Chief Osceola led a band that murdered a government agent. Another Seminole column wiped out US Major Francis Dade's entire relief force in the famous Dade Massacre. Florida was again in flames.

Before this conflict was over, the United States had fought its most costly Indian war, spending over $40 million and losing one thousand five hundred soldiers and many civilians. They battled an enemy one US officer called "bold, active and armed" and Black Seminoles "more desperate than Indians." In December 1836, General Sidney Thomas Jesup, who had recently assumed command of US forces, decided, "This, you may be assured, is a negro and not an Indian war."

General Jesup became the first commander to recognize the crucial role Black Seminoles played in the nation: "Throughout my operations I found the negroes the most active and determined warriors; and during the conferences with the Indian chief I ascertained that they exercised an almost controlling influence over them."

General Jesup first tried to destroy this alliance by assaulting Black Seminole villages and holding women and children hostage. He promised Creek mercenaries "plunder"—meaning captured people who could be sold as slaves. In two months, his troops seized 131 blacks, mostly women and children. When his men stormed Osceola's headquarters in January 1837, the chief's personal bodyguard was captured. Of the fifty-five men, fifty-two were black. Osceola escaped, but illness would end his life in a year.

By 1837 Osceola had become the leader of black and red resistance to US slaveholders. While the Seminole Nation as a whole showed signs of division, those who rode with Osceola, such as Wild Cat, were prepared to defend their black brothers and sisters to the death.

Since General Jesup's military operations had not captured one significant Seminole leader to negotiate with, he worried that his plans would backfire, that Black Seminoles would lead the nation in full-scale warfare. Worse still, he feared his policies might drive armed Black Seminoles to recruit plantation slaves and throw the countryside into disorder. He believed that Seminole warriors "have fought as long as they had life through the influence of the leading Negroes." For him the key to all negotiations became the Black Seminoles.

Under their own leaders, Negro Abraham and John Horse (or Cohia), and in concert with Chief Osceola and Wild Cat, Black Seminoles pursued their own strategy: Wear down US armed might until compromise was possible. Finally on March 6, 1837, both sides signed a treaty granting that Seminoles keep "their negroes, their *bona fide* property, [and] shall accompany them to the West." Jesup, despite pressure from US slaveholders and their political figures, felt he had no choice: "The negroes rule the Indians, and it is important that they should feel themselves secure; if they should become alarmed and hold out, the war will be resumed."

But General Jesup was not beyond more tricks. When Seminoles furnished hostages to seal the agreement, Jesup planned to let slave traders seize them. Hearing of this betrayal, Wild Cat and Black Seminole leader John Horse led a daring mission that rescued the hostages. At this point Seminole Blacks felt free to infiltrate US plantations urging a general uprising against both the US government and their masters.

"All is lost and principally by the influence of the Negroes," Jesup wrote. He now saw that "the two races . . . are identified in interests and feelings" and could not be separated. There was good reason to move Seminoles speedily to the frontier: "Should the Indians remain in this territory, the negroes among them will form a rallying point for runaway negroes from the adjacent states."

Despite his understanding of the racial alliance that dominated the Seminole Nation, General Jesup could not conclude peace. He continued to engage in cruel deceptions that violated the flag of truce, and he seized women and children as hostages. His actions left peace in doubt. In June 1837 he admitted as much: "We have at no former period in our history had to contend with so formidable an enemy. No Seminole proves false to his country, nor has a single instance ever occurred of a first-rate warrior having surrendered."

Between the General's understanding and his deceptive, militaristic approach lay a sea of gross strategic errors based on race: A US officer and his trained men should be able to defeat a ragged band of ex-slaves and their "savage" allies. No US officer should have to negotiate with such inferiors.

General Jesup faced a dilemma that could not lead to peace. He represented a country that thought Africans were spineless people fit for chains. When captured, such humans were not to be treated as gallant adversaries, but slave runaways. If he forgot these assumptions, his government in Washington and the slaveholders in his camps reminded him.

As the most knowledgeable representative of a giant country, Jesup wanted that victory whites told him was his. But his policies, tactics, and diplomacy were destined to place it beyond his reach.

WE ARE ALL LIVING AS IN ONE HOUSE

BY LATE 1837 THE US noose was tightening around the Seminole neck, but the nation showed no willingness to surrender. Those most determined to resist gathered around Osceola and Wild Cat. Still other Florida Seminoles, Africans, and Black Indians set up their own communities as they concluded the United States was untrustworthy. Some escaped to islands in the Caribbean, where slavery had been abolished since 1834.

Others remained in Florida and today some of their offspring claim the peninsula belongs to them, the descendants of the inhabitants who never surrendered.

CONCLUSION OF THE SEMINOLE WARS

IN THE FINAL MONTHS of his Florida effort, General Jesup resorted to full-scale deceptions and hostage seizures, and by the fall of 1837 he had captured King Philip and his Black Seminole

Wild Cat

son, John Philip. This brought forth King Philip's key son, Wild Cat, to negotiate. Riding a spirited horse, bearing a white crane's plume in his silver headband as a sign of peace, and accompanied by four chiefs, Wild Cat arrived to bargain for his father's and brother's release.

For a moment General Jesup wanted to seize him for his part in the recent hostage rescue success. Instead he decided to use him to organize a final peace conference. Wild Cat was sent forth bearing a white flag and asked to return with leading Seminoles.

His mission changed abruptly when he met his friend, John Horse. Both men were twenty-five, skilled warriors and shrewd negotiators. Their friendship would last for twenty years and revolve around their agreement that red and black Seminoles were blood sisters and brothers whom no foe could part. The tall Horse, elegantly attired, towered above the short, slight Wild Cat. Both had a tendency to drink too much, and Wild Cat let this habit interfere with his duties.

John Horse, Black Seminole leader

The two men saw there was something wrong with asking Seminole leaders to parlay with a foe that did not keep its word. John Horse suggested he alone should go to Fort Peyton to negotiate, and Wild Cat agreed. Horse was able to get Generals Jesup and Hernandez to agree to holding the conference near a Seminole camp. His own betrayal upset, Jesup wrote in his diary that "wherever John [Horse] Covallo was, foul play might be expected."

Then the two generals conspired to seize the entire Seminole peace mission. The Seminoles arrived with many leading figures and the seventy hostages they promised. Osceola was wearing a brightly colored outfit of a blue shirt, red leggings, and a red print shawl around his head, neck, and shoulders.

General Hernandez suddenly ordered the chiefs to deliver "all the Negroes taken from [US] citizens, at once." He made no mention of releasing King Philip and his son. As Seminoles stood shocked, Hernandez signaled and two hundred US Second Dragoons came out of forest hiding places, carbines aimed at Seminole hearts.

Prisoners were marched to the old jail at Fort Marion, and thrust into a cell thirty-three-by-eighteen feet to await deportation to Arkansas. Osceola, probably ill with the fever that would soon take his life, slumped in a corner. Wild Cat, John Horse at his side, took command of plans for a breakout.

While Generals Jesup and Hernandez congratulated themselves on a masterful truce violation that captured a dozen Seminole leaders, their prisoners were tearing at a rusted bar blocking a hole atop their eighteen-foot high cell. "We resolved to make our escape or die in the attempt," Wild Cat later wrote. Since the prisoners appeared to accept their fate, a US medical corpsman wrote, "The Indians are perfectly secure and do not dream of escape."

It was weeks before Wild Cat, John Horse, and the others weakened the huge iron bar that blocked the hole. Osceola, at thirty-four, his life slipping fast, took no part. When a delegation of Cherokees came in to convince the Seminoles to surrender, Osceola weakly waved "no." During this time Wild Cat's youngest and oldest brothers were also captured and thrown in the cell.

Finally, the bar was loosened, and one night twenty Seminoles, including two women, were led to freedom by Wild Cat and John Horse. For five days, Wild Cat recalled, they lived "on roots and berries." On the fifth day they reached friends who supplied them with food, clothing, and new weapons. "I'd rather be killed by a white man in Florida, than die in Arkansas," Wild Cat later wrote.

Colonel Zachary Taylor raced after the fugitives with 70 Delaware Indians, 180 Tennessee volunteer sharpshooters and 800 US soldiers. By the time Taylor's huge force approached Lake Okeechobee the day before Christmas, dozens of Seminole warriors were hiding in the tall grass or perched in trees.

The first shot had hardly been fired when the Delawares deserted. Tennessee riflemen plunged ahead intending to wipe out the Seminoles and a withering fire brought down their commissioned officers and then their noncommissioned officers. The Tennesseeans fled.

When the US regulars were ordered forward, pinpoint accurate fire brought down, according to Colonel Taylor, "every officer, with one exception, as well as most of the noncommissioned officers" and left "but four . . . untouched."

Knowing they were no match for hundreds of soldiers, the Seminoles retreated to waiting canoes and made their escape. On Christmas Day Colonel Taylor counted 28 US dead and 112 wounded, and only ten Seminoles dead.

The strongest country in the New World had received a stunning defeat at the hands of a small band of Black Indian guerrilla fighters. The battle of Lake Okeechobee became the most decisive upset the United States suffered in more than four decades of warfare in Florida. But, since the Seminoles had finally abandoned the battle scene, Colonel Taylor claimed a victory.

To seek revenge, a furious General Jesup mounted up and rode his troops out, but fared little better than Taylor in defeating the Seminoles. Finally, Jesup solemnly promised to negotiate a peace that permitted all Seminoles to migrate together to the Indian Territory in Arkansas and Oklahoma. But he was too

Many Florida Seminoles claimed they were never defeated by or surrendered to the US.

late. In May 1838 Jesup was recalled to Washington, his military and peace campaigns a failure. Zachary Taylor, now a brigadier general, assumed the US command in Florida.

It was not until General Worth and 1841 that peace finally came to most of Florida's lush battlefields. "Ten resolute Negroes, with a knowledge of the country, are sufficient to desolate the frontier, from one extent to another," General Worth was told. Not wishing to preside over that dread possibility, he advocated removing all Seminoles before "they become a resort for runaways" and ignite a war "quadruplicate in time and treasure than that now waged." By 1843 most of the Seminole Nation, including five hundred African Americans, had reached the Indian Territory.

But war in Florida among Seminole holdouts randomly flared up like a fire that never died. Although in 1844 Wild Cat,

John Horse, and other chiefs had traveled to the White House to meet with President Polk, warfare again erupted in the early 1850s and did not end until 1858. For more than forty years men and women in Florida had died trying to live free.

In 1858 a *Harper's Weekly* reporter wrote of a familiar sight:

> The negro slaves are, in fact, the masters of their own red owners. . . . The negroes were the master spirits, as well as the immediate occasion, of the Florida wars. They openly refused to follow their masters if they removed to Arkansas; it was not until they capitulated that the Seminoles ever thought of emigrating.

LIFE IN THE INDIAN TERRITORY

SEMINOLES ARRIVED IN THE Indian Territory west of the Mississippi to find themselves at the mercy of a familiar set of enemies. As one of the Five Nations, they were located on land dominated by the Creek Nation. These ancient foes bitterly resented them for abandoning the old confederation. Surrounded by Creeks, Chickasaws, Cherokees, Choctaws, and whites who practiced a cruel bondage over black people, Seminoles felt pressure at every turn.

The US government spent only three and a half cents a day to feed and clothe each Seminole, and there was little work at first. Wild Cat and John Horse labored hard to feed their people and keep up their sagging spirits. Worst of all, Seminoles became targets of slavehunting raiders, particularly Creeks and whites.

Only the reputation of their fighting men kept the nation from being destroyed.

Seminoles were finally given their own section of land, on which they grew crops of corn and rice. These they sold at a good profit. Though they soon convinced their Indian agent they were "high-minded, open, candid and brave people," they were not able to persuade the government to provide them with a school.

In 1849 a pro-slavery faction defeated Wild Cat's bid to lead the nation. For Wild Cat and the Black Seminoles, more was at stake than an election. Once he had envisioned a unity among all red and black people in the southwest, and now he could barely protect his own band of mixed Seminoles.

In 1846, Wild Cat had visited Texas three times to meet Kickapoos, Lipans, Apaches, and Tonkawas to discuss his plans. They had listened politely and had not turned him down. Two years later Wild Cat had urged the militaristic Plains Nations to join his Seminoles against Creek, white, and other slavehunters. They did not offer to help.

Little more is known about his grand design than that Wild Cat hoped to establish a military colony for oppressed Indian and black people. He wanted to recruit from the Five Nations, from Texas and Arkansas plantations, and perhaps elsewhere once his movement gained momentum. Historian Kenneth W. Porter has written: "Wild Cat's ambitions in some respects exceeded those of King Philip, Pontiac and Tecumseh, for he envisioned a union of half a dozen linguistic groups and two races."

In late 1849, the Wild Cat Seminole party received another blow. The US attorney general ruled that Black Seminoles were still slaves under US law. These veterans of many battles to live as a people quietly gathered up and loaded their rifles. Chief John Horse founded the town of Wewoka, moved his families there, and had his crack scouts patrol its boundaries. Intruders, including any who demanded surrender of "slaves," were turned away.

The final blow for the Wild Cat band came when Creeks and US whites demanded that Black Seminoles surrender their guns. At harvest time in 1849, Wild Cat, John Horse, and their followers saddled up and rode toward Mexico. In one night hundreds of Seminoles left the Indian Territory and headed toward the Rio Grande. The United States was moving swiftly toward armed conflict over slavery, and the Seminole Nation was the first to catch fire.

At the Mexican border Seminole men ferried their women and children across the Rio Grande at Eagle Pass. The men crossed at dawn as armed pursuers galloped into sight and began firing. It was the summer of 1850 and the United States was poised for a decade of bitter conflict over slavery, and finally a war that would pit brother against brother. Becky Simmons, one of the first to cross the river that fateful night, recalled how relieved she was to get "away from de American race people."

At each step of the way to becoming a peaceful agricultural nation, Black Seminoles had been blocked by those seeking slaves. Each time Seminole military strength saved them. Would Mexico finally offer a Seminole Nation peace and land?

The Wild Cat exodus numbered about eight hundred people. Wild Cat also brought some Cherokee and Creek slaves to learn his route to the Rio Grande, and then guide back others. When Wild Cat returned to the Indian Territory in September 1850, he discovered that Black Seminoles who had remained behind were being kidnapped daily by slavehunters.

Creeks, fearful that Wild Cat now meant to lead off their slaves, tried to arrest him. The cagey chief simply announced he had a thousand Kickapoos and others nearby and ready to defend him, and about six hundred armed Creeks turned around and went home.

TWENTY YEARS IN MEXICO

WILD CAT NEGOTIATED FOR his sovereign nation with President Santa Ana of Mexico. In return for Mexican Army pay and some farmland for their families, Seminole men agreed to serve as "military colonists" along the turbulent Rio Grande border. They dug in at Coahuila province; Wild Cat located below Piedras Negras, and John Horse above it. Their young men became part of Mexico's armed forces, and Wild Cat was appointed a judge and commissioned a colonel.

Seminoles arrived in a country that had ended slavery in 1829 and had welcomed slave fugitives ever since. Some three thousand US blacks lived peacefully in Mexico, most of them far from the Rio Grande border. Periodically, slavehunting

Red and Black Seminoles in Florida retained their cultural traditions as shown in this early twentieth-century marriage ceremony.

posses plunged across the river to seize black people for sale back home. Some Mexican politicians conspired with these desperadoes, the better to finance their political campaigns.

Seminole families had hardly settled down when in 1851 US outlaw John "Rip" Ford rode into Mexico with a band of four hundred men. Wild Cat and John Horse were called upon to drive out these former Texas Rangers and unemployed Texans. Sixty Seminole fighters drove back the Texans without a casualty. Pleased Mexican officials thanked the Seminoles as "faithful and useful . . . in military operations" and complimented them as "industrious workers."

Relations between Mexico and the United States were uneasy and the borderlands dangerous. When John Horse rode to US Fort Duncan to reclaim a horse, he was seized and thrown out by laughing US infantrymen. That year, when the chief was wounded during a shoot-out at Piedras Negras, he was handcuffed and dragged across the border by US ruffians. Wild Cat ransomed Horse for $500, paying in gold stained with blood.

Wild Cat and John Horse worked hard at building good relations with the Mexicans. Black Seminole Rosa Fay remembered: "John Horse would never even let the little children fight with the Mexican children, because he said, 'When we came, fleeing slavery, Mexico was a land of freedom and the Mexicans spread out their arms to us.'"

When Mexicans found fault with Seminole failures to follow army orders, they had a point. Wild Cat and John Horse regularly disregarded orders they considered wrong. Mexican officials complained about Seminole lack of discipline and attention to their authority. But they also found this unruly strike force was "always triumphant."

As Seminole fighting men achieved a reputation far and wide for toughness, new recruits—slave runaways from Texas, Black Mexicans, Indian Territory blacks—flocked to their villages. For the nation's elders, the dream of a farming community still remained the great goal.

In 1855 another white invasion force crossed the Rio Grande and captured Piedras Negras. Worried Mexican officials asked Wild Cat and John Horse to assist the Mexican Army. The US forces became bottled up in the city and got a hotter reception than anyone planned when Piedras Negras caught fire. This band of slavehunters, desperadoes, and young men out for fun were lucky to escape back across the Rio Grande.

In 1856 the issue of Seminole refusal to take sides in Mexican politics came up sharply. The ruler of Coahuila ordered John Horse's troops into combat against a political rival. Horse refused. Rosa Fay remembered his position: "'Here we are,' John Horse would say, 'all living as in one house. How can I take up a gun and kill you, who are my brother, or how can I take up a gun for you and kill that other man, who is also my brother.'"

To explain his decision Chief Horse led a delegation of Seminoles to Mexico City. It was not treason, he said, but neutrality that guided Seminole thinking and action. He and the Seminoles were reprimanded for failing "to render profound respect to the public authorities and to obey their orders." But they were also excused from "taking part in our political dissensions."

Chief Horse's considerable diplomatic skills proved as effective as his military ones. He did not know then that within a year he would need all his personal strength as well.

In late 1856, the United States declared that Seminoles were not a part of the Creek Nation, subject to its laws, but independent. This was the signal some of Wild Cat's band had been waiting for, and they packed up for the Indian Territory. Black Seminoles, who would never return to a land of bondage, remained with Wild Cat and some of his followers in Mexico.

Then, in January 1857, nature dealt the remaining Seminoles a cruel blow when smallpox swept through their villages leaving fifty dead. Panicky men and women fled to the woods and hills while others prayed for deliverance. For some, it was a signal that Mexico was more dangerous than the United States. Black Seminoles, with an African immunity, were spared. But the plague carried off Wild Cat, at forty-five, whose force and wisdom had held his nation together. Becky Simmons recalled the mourning of her people: "Later Wild Cat took sick with de pox and he die. We all was crying fur we done lost him. He was so good."

After Wild Cat's death, his remaining red followers began to trickle back to the Indian Territory. The Black Seminoles were now alone. Becky Simmons remembered, "John Horse . . . [became] our next head man, but dem others been gone back to de territory."

As soldiers guarding the Rio Grande against rustlers and assorted desperadoes of every shade, the Black Seminoles rolled up an impressive record. In 20 battles they captured 432 horses and mules and killed 38 intruders. Not a single Seminole was killed or wounded. Some considered this a miracle.

But the greatest accomplishment of all was the preservation of their nation as they moved from one country to another.

THAT YOU KNOW WHO WE ARE

FOR THE BLACK SEMINOLE Nation the Fourth of July, 1870, proved a memorable day. For the white citizens of southern Texas it was a day few would ever forget. Scores of shabbily dressed Seminoles, some on horses carrying infants, and others on foot with their belongings and children, arrived at US Fort Duncan. Led by Snake Warrior, subchief to John Horse, they were the first of three waves of Seminole immigrants to arrive from Mexico over the next eighteen months.

The US Army had sent Captain Frank Perry to Mexico to negotiate an agreement with the Black Nation. In return for its young men serving as scouts for the army, families would be provided food, necessities, and eventually good farming land.

Most remarkable is that a Black Nation negotiated its entrance into the United States by formal treaty. It then arrived intact as a nation, together with its reigning monarch, Chief John Horse.

For both Seminoles and the US Army, this could not have been an easy decision. Black people were voluntarily returning to a country that enslaved their ancestors and then sent armies to crush those who fled their chains. On the army's side, it was hiring men as scouts whom it could not defeat in a century of warfare.

What crucial changes had taken place by 1870 that would make allies of two sworn adversaries? First, the Civil War had ended slavery in the United States, and black people now were forever free. Three Amendments to the Constitution promised equality to ex-slaves, and black men were voting and being elected to office in Texas and nine other southern states. A new day was dawning.

The US Army faced hazardous problems in Texas, and these Black Seminole fighters were a powerful answer. Four thousand six hundred and twelve US soldiers and officers had to protect 267,339 square miles of mayhem, and guard a restless Rio Grande border. Comanches, Kiowas, Apaches, and various US and Mexican bandit gangs could out-ride and out-fox the Army almost every time.

Worse still, after each surprise, the Army failed miserably at locating or inflicting much damage on their highly mobile foes. This was more than a military problem. For politicians back home victories in the West made good reading for voters and defeats were intolerable.

The Army had a civilian problem as well. Behind their blue-coated backs stood hostile, unreformed southern rebels, who hated the sight of Yankees and their uniforms. When bluecoats battled either Indians or outlaws, it was unclear which side white Texans would cheer.

Somewhere out there, in front of the frontier US Army forts stood groups of cagey native desert fighters the soldiers in blue could not detect, track, or defeat. The Seminole Negro Indian Scouts, as they came to be called in official US records, were hired to even the battle odds.

Major Zenas A. Bliss, desperate for good scouts, sent Captain Perry off to Mexico to sign up these peerless warriors. Seminoles remembered signing this "treaty" with Perry, but the piece of paper, which soon became a bone of contention, disappeared.

THE SEMINOLE NEGRO INDIAN SCOUTS

THE BLACK SEMINOLE PEOPLE arrived on the US side of the Rio Grande like typical immigrants, hoping for their share of iron pots, warm blankets, and good rifles. Like most immigrants to the United States, they pined for a piece of land they could call their own. Perhaps they assumed that since the US government was prepared to treat them fairly, so would its citizens. They tried to wash the past from their minds and be prepared to enjoy the American Dream.

Texas, as a hotbed of secessionist, racist sentiment, was not about to open its arms to a fiercely independent Black Indian population. People of their color had recently been a salable item in Texas, and most whites regretted this was no longer true. But here was an arrogant, ragged band of Black Indians asking to be treated with respect. This proved too much for white Texans.

The Texas borderlands in the 1870s boasted a savage bloodletting all its own. Discharged Confederate veterans, furious

This photograph of the Seminole Negro Indian scouts was taken in 1889, probably in Texas.

about defeat and the emancipation of their slaves, were still armed and dangerous. Unemployed, they easily became desperadoes spoiling for a fight. This was not a land for the fainthearted or for families with women and children.

The infamous "King" Fisher outlaw gang dominated the Eagle Pass region near Fort Duncan. Cattle-rustling was big business in those parts and John "King" Fisher, handsome and suave, became the most significant political figure in the region. He was not a man you wanted to harbor an active dislike of you.

Almost from the arrival of the Seminole Nation, Fisher decided to challenge Chief John Horse and his men. His gang may have served as the violent cutting edge for whites who wanted the lands Seminoles had settled.

Though they did not suspect it at first, this last great effort by the Black Seminole people to find peace and land had entered an explosive phase.

Seminole life in Texas began simply enough with seasoned Seminole scouts being trained by green West Point graduates unfamiliar with desert warfare or Seminole ways. The recruits were young men of African or mixed Black Indian ancestry in their late teens or early twenties. One, Jim Miller, was said to have "looked white and acted Indian."

In dress, manners, and skills, Seminole men were like Plains Indians. As desert fighters and trackers, they were probably the finest soldiers the US Army ever sent into the field. With their unique skills and record of triumphs over any who crossed their path, they must have approached their new assignment brimming with confidence.

They could maneuver their steeds with grace and wield their rifles with accuracy from the saddle. In Mexico they had used slow, muzzle-loading guns. Now the United States handed them Spencer carbines, and then the fine Sharps carbines that allowed for smoother, faster loading and firing than any they had ever seen.

The first Seminole-Army tensions began during basic training as white officers tried to impose discipline on these young veterans. These were not eager, inexperienced recruits ready to swallow the army's many rules and regulations. Their monarch had negotiated their hiring as a representative of a sovereign nation. They expected respect.

For their white officers, shock probably came the first time the scouts lined up. Facing US army officers were not neatly dressed, obedient raw recruits, but scruffy men sporting Indian war bonnets, sometimes with buffalo horns. The earliest army reports praise the scouts' fighting abilities but bemoan their appearance—"very poor"—and their clothing—"good enough for Indians."

Lieutenant
John L. Bullis

During the training period, Chief John Horse and his military commander, Snake Warrior, tried to mediate between their scouts and the army brass. The task of finding an officer who could command them and gain their respect was not solved for two years.

The job was finally handed to a young white lieutenant from New York, John L. Bullis. A man of striking contradictions and an unconventional soldier, he proved as tough as his men. Bullis was a Quaker who enlisted as a Union private in the Civil War. As an officer he volunteered to lead black troops. Now filled with traditional army training, he was picked to command the most unorthodox fighting force the United States had ever handed rifles.

Clearly a man willing to charge uphill, Bullis had met and married Alicia Rodriguez, a Mexican woman. In Texas, in 1872, this was considered as outrageous as leading Black Indians.

The strong relationship that developed between the short, slight, wiry officer and his scouts made their work unusually effective. Bible in hand, Bullis was invited to Seminole villages to perform marriages and baptisms. Since their own marriage probably did not win them many friends at the fort, the couple may have spent considerable time with Seminoles.

On the trail Bullis and his scouts quickly became a fighting fist, bold and loyal, risking death for each other. Scout Joseph Philips recalled the relationship in these words:

> The Scouts thought a lot of Bullis. Lieutenant Bullis was the only officer that ever did stay the longest with us. That fella suffer just like we-all did out in de woods. He was a good man. He was an Injun fighter. He was tuff. He didn't care how big a bunch dey was, he went into 'em every time, but he look out for his men. His men was on equality, too. He didn't stand and say, "Go yonder;" he would say "Come on boys, let's go get 'em."

Under Bullis's careful guidance, the Seminole Negro Indian Scouts drove their incomparable skills into the battle against crime in Texas. They could pick up a trail three weeks old, track foes who believed they had eluded all pursuers, and then surprise a target when least expected. On the trail they lived by uncovering hidden springs and eating the rattlesnakes they caught.

They also remained alive by keeping a sharp eye on each other. On April 25, 1875, Bullis, Sergeant John Ward, Trumpeter

Isaac Payne, and Private Pompey Factor were tracking a party of twenty-five Comanche rustlers. They came on their quarry and seventy-five stolen horses near the Pecos River at Eagles' Nest. With a daring that bordered on foolishness, the four men challenged the twenty-five.

When the Comanche realized they faced only four, they charged, their Winchester rifle fire driving the scouts back toward their horses. As the Seminoles galloped off, Sergeant Ward turned and saw that Bullis had fallen from his mount and Comanches were closing in on him.

"We can't leave the Lieutenant, boys," Ward shouted and the three scouts wheeled their horses and raced back. As Ward reached Bullis, a bullet cut his carbine sling and another shattered his rifle stock. He reached down and pulled Bullis up on his horse, and the two galloped away, bullets whizzing past them. "I . . . just saved my hair by jumping on my Sergeant's horse, back of him," Bullis later wrote.

Bullis formally requested that his men each receive the Congressional Medal of Honor. His request was honored and for their valor the three received the highest US military decoration.

END OF A MISSION

NO AMOUNT OF PRAISE or medals won the Black Seminole Nation its dream of land and a peaceful life. Repeatedly Chief John Horse led delegations to military authorities and handed in petitions signed by his people. He asked for adherence to treaty obligations, but there was no copy of the disputed treaty.

After three years Seminoles were still squatting on US

military reservations at Fort Duncan and Fort Clark close to the Rio Grande. The War Department said it had no land to offer them, and the Department of the Interior claimed they were not entitled to lands granted Indians.

Chief John Horse gathered letters of support from Lieutenant Bullis, Major Bliss, General C. C. Auger (commander, Department of Texas), and General Philip Sheridan, Civil War hero. Neither petitions, pleas, nor letters of support melted any bureaucratic hearts in Washington.

To make matters worse, the army high command issued orders that cut Seminole rations. Food and necessities for about fifty scouts were spread among three hundred men, women, and children. Soon a proud nation was reduced to foraging for food, stealing stray cattle, and taking servant jobs in white homes. Some scouts left for Mexico with their families, and their places were taken by eager African Americans, Mexican Seminoles, and other red and black Indians.

As a fighting unit the Seminole Negro Indian Scouts rolled up an impressive record guarding the Texas frontier against intruders. By a miracle they suffered no casualties. Scout Bill Daniels believed that when "you are fighting for the right . . . God will spread His hand over you."

But there was no one to protect the Seminoles from the white Texans they guarded. John "King" Fisher made it his goal to drive off the Black Seminoles and assassinate their monarch, John Horse. Besides resenting the proud black fighters, he probably objected to the war on crime they fought in the Eagle Pass region where his rustler gang roamed.

Fisher boasted he had killed a man for every year of his life "not counting Mexicans." With their carbines and six-shooters, his outlaws dominated politics, business, and life in the region.

By Christmas 1874, trouble between King Fisher's desperadoes and the Seminoles boiled over. There was a shoot-out in a Bracketville saloon and Corporal George Washington, Chief Horse's nephew, was fatally wounded in the stomach. Another bullet creased King Fisher's scalp, leaving him shaken but even more determined to settle matters with guns.

To halt the bloodshed before it became open warfare, the army moved the Black Seminole Nation to Fort Clark, which was farther from Bracketville than Fort Duncan. But if anyone believed mere distance would satisfy the outlaws, they were wrong.

The Seminoles found farming and living conditions at Fort Clark more pleasant than Fort Duncan. But no sooner had they settled down than they learned that Kinney County whites wanted their new land. And the King Fisher gang stood ready to push any dispute with Black Seminoles into a shooting war.

In the spring of 1876, Chief Horse and scout Titus Payne were peacefully riding near an army hospital when they were shot from an ambush. Payne was dead by the time he hit the ground. John Horse was badly wounded, as was his horse, American. But American was able to pull the injured chief to safety, probably saving his life.

By now Seminoles may have felt themselves at sea among weak friends and deadly enemies. Local whites wanted them removed from lands they farmed and local outlaws wanted them dead. The army paid for their services as scouts but drastically reduced their rations and refused to grant them land promised in a treaty. Their friends, from powerful generals down, signed their petitions, but no one in Washington cared. Seminole fighting men could defeat any foe, but no one could protect innocent people from cowardly ambushes.

By this time a sturdy nation had become deeply divided over their stay in the United States. Some families gave up and returned to Mexico.

For many huddling in the temporary village outside Fort Clark, the last straw came during the early morning of a New Year's Eve dance in 1877. A local sheriff and his deputies rode out to arrest Adam Payne in connection with the murder of an African American soldier.

Payne had a reputation as a tough man and had earned a Congressional Medal of Honor. The sheriff may have planned his next move or just lost his courage. At any rate he did not arrest

Payne, but blasted him from behind with a shotgun—at such close range that Payne's clothes caught fire.

This pointless violence sent shock waves through the entire community, and five scouts, led by Pompey Factor, immediately packed up and rode off to the Rio Grande.

Private Pompey Factor

They paused only to wash the dust of Texas from their horses' hooves, and then continued on into Mexico.

The majority of the scouts remained loyal if not to the US government, at least to Bullis and their jobs. New recruits were no longer from the original Black Seminole Nation. More and more they came from Texas African Americans, former black US soldiers, and black Mexicans.

By 1882 Bullis and his scouts had virtually pacified a terrifying no man's land. That year a dozen army expeditions from Texas Army posts covered 3,662 miles and found no criminal raiders of any kind. In eleven years, twenty-six expeditions, and twelve major engagements, Bullis and his desert fighters had not lost a man in battle or had one seriously wounded.

They frightened off the most dangerous scorpions and brought law and order to a land known for marauding killers. Bullis was honored as "The Friend of the Frontier" by Texans, and later became a brigadier general in the army. He was presented with two handsome swords by appreciative local citizens and listed in *Who Was Who in America*. He was once called "the greatest Indian fighter in the history of the United States Army."

His wife, Alicia, died young, and Bullis remarried and settled down in San Antonio. He died in 1911 of a heart attack.

DEATH OF A NATION

THE BRAVE SEMINOLE NEGRO Indian Scouts did not share in this glory. Although the unit was not formally dissolved until 1914, it had lost heart earlier, on the night Adam Payne was murdered.

In 1882 an aging John Horse undertook a final mission for his land-hungry people. He rode his horse American out of Texas into Mexico. According to one of his followers, he was "hunting for a place to live, for a home—he was always doing that." The gracious reigning Seminole monarch was never seen again.

For a piece of the American Dream, he and his people had pinned their hopes on a return to a United States free of slavery. Some had given their last full measure of devotion, and none had received their due or their land.

Pompey Factor as a young private helped save the life of Lieutenant Bullis, and received the Medal of Honor. But years later he could not even get an army pension. In his late seventies and still carrying the empty case that once held his medal, he asked a Texas lawyer to plead his case before the Army brass. It was no use. The Army responded that it had no record of his service.

Two years later, in 1928, Pompey Factor died and was buried in Bracketville, Texas. His funeral expenses of $86.40 were paid by a friend because he died penniless and without an army pension.

Today the remaining members of the Black Seminole Nation are distributed on both sides of the Rio Grande border near Eagle Pass, scene of their greatest triumphs and losses. They are largely part of the region's dark poor, their historic valor still unrecognized.

There is no monument to Seminole courage and audacity anywhere in this country. In 1970 a Seminole Negro Indian graveyard outside Bracketville was set aside to mark the final resting place of Pompey Factor, Isaac Payne, Adam Payne, and other people who had no rest while they were alive. They should have earned more than that late gesture to their fallen heroes.

Is there any group in history that, beginning before 1776 and stretching from one generation into the next for more than a century—and reaching from Florida's marshlands to Texas's deserts—fought harder for liberty and justice in the Americas?

The last word about the Black Seminole Nation should rest with its historic figure, John Horse. In December 1873 he and Snake Warrior walked into General Augur's office and entered a plea for "my people" to "have a home." In his most diplomatic language the chief reminded the general he had fought almost a dozen US generals in Florida. He had negotiated with General Taylor who became a US president and with President James Polk in Washington.

Graves of brothers Adam and Isaac Payne, in Bracketville, Texas, in the 1980s.

Still identifying himself as part of "the Seminole Wild Cat Party," his words were taken down by an Army scribe and sent on to the adjutant general in Washington. John Horse's oral petition is on file in the National Archives. This is part of what he said:

> . . . I want full rations for my people, please if so granted, and I like to have the Mexicans who are intermarried with my people, and which are with us, and good men, may be enlisted for scouting.
>
> . . . I say for my people that the President of the United States may grant us what the Fathers before God have promised us; and I come here, General Augur, to present you all this, that you know who we are.
>
> General, I come here to make a new treaty, and the wish I ask for please grant Sir; the same time I want to see all my children have their right, as I brought them all here. . . .
>
> We come here not to tell a lie, but to tell the whole truth, and that you do all for us you can to have a home. . . .
>
> *John Horse*
> his *X* mark

HE WAS OUR GO-BETWEEN

FOR THE EARLIEST EUROPEAN colonists, the Americas were truly a land of opportunity. They came from a continent torn with religious strife. Kings, nobles, and merchants regularly dragged their people into land and sea wars. The plight of ordinary men and women was terrible. About 2 percent of the population owned 95 percent of the land. Common folk wallowed in poverty and want, without hope or security. They were forced into labor battalions or conscript armies.

Everywhere a rigid intolerance held sway. Europeans lived by a rural British slogan: "He's a stranger, hit him on the head!"

Europeans greeted the people of the Americas with hostility and a lust for profit. In dealing with non-Christians, they saw little reason to observe common rules of fair play, and rarely did. They tramped into the American wilderness with a Bible, a musket, and a diplomacy that knew no rules.

Some Africans became more than peacemakers, negotiators, and bridges between cultures in the wilderness. They began to identify with their new friends of the hills, streams, and mountains. A few wrote unheralded chapters in New World diplomacy.

ESTEVANICO

IT IS AN IRONY that the first explorer from the Old World to enter Arizona and New Mexico's free, vast expanses was himself a slave. But Estevanico was a highly unusual individual who left a confused legacy. Even his name poses a question. Since he was called Estevanico or Little Stephen, was he a tall, even gigantic "Little Stephen," or an unusually small "Little Stephen"?

Not too much is known of his early life. Born in Azamore, Morocco, around 1500, he was probably made captive as a teenager when Portugal's King Manoel seized the city in 1513. His record is a blank until June 17, 1527. Then he emerged as a bearded young man, the slave of a Spaniard, Andrés Dorantes, as the two board a ship at Sanlúcar de Barrameda, Spain, for the New World.

The Spaniard and the Moroccan had hardly landed in exotic Hispaniola when they joined an expedition to explore Florida. In 1528 King Ferdinand ordered the exploration and his newly appointed governor of Florida, Pánfilo de Narváez, personally led it.

Some five hundred Spaniards and their African slaves set out on an adventure none would ever forget. From the moment of their first landing at Sarasota Bay the effort skidded toward catastrophe. They quickly ran out of food and then patience.

Spaniards, used to a pleasantly warm climate, had to contend with tropical rainstorms, wild animals, jungles, and quicksand. Starvation drove desperate men toward madness. Some ran off seeking salvation in the treacherous countryside, others prayed in vain and many died hungry and lost.

By the time the explorers reached a Native American village they counted only eighty survivors. But calamities had just begun. While the exhausted men rested, disease struck, leaving only fifteen survivors. Narváez and his men named this place "Misfortune Island" and pushed on.

Bad luck continued to stalk the foreigners. Death carried off Narváez and, one by one, most of the others. Soon of the original five hundred adventurers only Andrés Dorantes, Estevanico, Cabeza de Vaca, and one other Spaniard remained alive.

Alone in a terrifying land they barely understood, the four shared hardship and want. At one point they were made slaves of separate Indian Nations, but during a meeting of their masters, they made good an escape. They would spend eight years wandering.

A diary of their sojourn was kept by their leader, Cabeza de Vaca. It told of Estevanico's crucial role whenever Indians appeared. He posed as a medicine man and magic healer, and the other three followed his lead. Estevanico found success reciting improvised prayers and making signs over ill and dying Indians. For this service the four were rewarded with food, water, and directions. As the most skilled magic healer, Estevanico was able to gain valuable information and necessities from grateful Native Americans.

Further, as they made their way from one native village to

another, the African picked up languages from and instilled confidence in those he met. De Vaca's account records that it was Estevanico who "was our go-between; he informed himself about the ways we wished to take, what towns there were, and the matters we desired to know."

By now Estevanico was beginning to hear, along with other information, wild tales about rich Cibola, or "The Seven Cities of Gold." The Spaniards shared the excitement when Indians insisted that somewhere north of Mexico lay a city made of gold and silver. This was the glittering wealth Spain had hoped to find in the New World.

In 1536 the four shabby survivors staggered into Spanish headquarters in Mexico. They brought with them the first great folk myth of the Americas—the tale of Cibola. After the three

In this mural by Jay Datus, Estevanico is shown on his mission to find the "Seven Cities of Gold."

Spaniards recovered from their ordeal and regained some weight, they left for Spain. Not even the lure of gold and silver could hold them.

Estevanico did not have that choice, and he was sold to the Viceroy of Hispaniola, Antonio de Mendoza. The governor kept his slave guest talking about Cibola's riches, and Estevanico produced some bright metal objects natives had given him to claim that smelting was an art practiced in Cibola.

In 1538 Governor Mendoza organized an expedition to discover this land of great wealth and picked Father Marcos de Niza, a Franciscan friar, to lead it. Estevanico was his advance scout and advisor.

The African was sent ahead with a few Indians and two greyhounds and was directed to send back accounts of his progress toward Cibola. The closer he came or the more information he gathered, the faster he would contact Father de Niza. The unusual method of communication chosen by the priest was a cross. The closer Estevanico came to Cibola, the larger the cross to be sent back.

Heading northwest from Mexico, Estevanico employed his experience as a translator and his guise as a medicine man. He carried a large gourd decorated with a string of bells and one red and one white feather to symbolize a search for peace and friendship. Indian men and women—as many as three hundred—joined his party and adorned him with jewelry and gifts.

Estevanico began to send back crosses to indicate progress, each larger than the last. His Indian messengers told Father de Niza of his scout's large following and rapid strides. Enthusiasm mounted as the priest urged a faster pace to reach Cibola, just behind Estevanico.

Then, suddenly, there was no word from the African—no messengers, no crosses. The rest of the expedition stopped and waited tensely. Finally, two wounded Indians staggered into the priest's camp. They told a story of terror, death, and sorrow. Estevanico and his followers were approaching a village near Cibola when they were attacked. The party scattered, some captured, others slain.

Estevanico? "We think they have shot him to death," the Indians said. "We are the only survivors."

The story of Estevanico here becomes conjecture and argument. Some historians, unfriendly toward the African, claim he abused Indian women and cheated their men, so he was murdered. One scholar believes Estevanico died for claiming to represent a powerful white country to Indians. Some historians have wondered if the young slave saw an opportunity for freedom and took it.

Perhaps he created a clever cover story—"We think they have shot him to death"—and made good his escape.

The Zuñi Nation, whose pueblos he was approaching at the end, told a folk legend into the twentieth century about a brave Black Mexican—a large man, with "chilli [thick] lips" who was "killed by our ancestors."

No one ever found the Seven Cities of Gold, but Estevanico's efforts led to the first thorough exploration of the American southwest by Coronado and others. The African's command of languages, his ability to win Native Americans' confidence, stand in sharp contrast to the brutality of European adventurers. Bold and persuasive, and with some tricks up his sleeve, Estevanico succeeded mainly through a sensitive human touch.

⇥ ⇤

IT IS UNCLEAR WHETHER Estevanico lived happily with the native people of Arizona or New Mexico or died at their hands. The story of a fur trapper named Du Sable leaves no doubt that this handsome black Frenchman married into and remained a good friend of the Illinois Indians.

He also maneuvered with the skill of an experienced diplomat as Illinois slipped from French to British to US control. His personal charm and diplomacy kept him from being jailed as an enemy agent and won him powerful white and Indian allies.

There are gaps in his early life. Du Sable was born somewhere in the Caribbean in 1745 to a French sailor father and an African slave woman. Sent to Paris for an education, he ended up in the Illinois Territory in 1779. With him came twenty-three French art treasures and a desire to become a fur trapper.

As a Frenchman in a land recently taken by the British, Du Sable fell under suspicion. On July 4, 1779, a British officer complained he "was much in the interest of the French" and Du Sable was arrested for "treasonable intercourse with the enemy." He managed to escape only to be arrested again. This time he so impressed British Governor Patrick Sinclair that Du Sable was released and for five years placed in charge of a settlement on the St. Charles River.

Du Sable had no difficulty in persuading local Indians he was a friend. It took much longer for white Chicagoans to recognize that Du Sable was their city's founder.

Du Sable entered the fur trading business and married a Potawatomi woman named Catherine. Their many friends included Chief Pontiac and Daniel Boone. One can only wonder

what rough frontiersmen and Indians thought when they first entered the Du Sable home and saw its display of French works of art. The couple also purchased and developed some eight hundred acres of land in Peoria, but Chicago was their great love and they lived there for sixteen years.

Their trading post became prosperous and the Du Sables soon had a son and a daughter. Centrally located, their store and home attracted many trappers and swelled to include a forty by twenty-foot log cabin, a bakehouse, a dairy, a smoke house, a poultry house; a workshop, a barn, and a mill. Du Sable made a living as a trader, but was also a miller, a cooper, and a farmer.

The Du Sables became devout Catholics and in 1798 were formally married in a church ceremony. They were delighted when, two years later, their daughter married another Frenchman in a Catholic ceremony.

Jean and Catherine, although doing well, sold off twenty-one of his French paintings, perhaps to finance his next career move. He announced his candidacy for chief of a local Indian Nation at Mackinac, but he lost the election.

As the couple grew older they decided to sell their Chicago home and move in with their daughter's new family in St. Charles, Missouri. For the property and houses alone, they received $1200, and they also sold thirty head of cattle, thirty-eight pigs, two mules, and many chickens.

When Catherine died in 1800, the founder of Chicago began to worry about his future. He did not want to die penniless or to be buried in any but a Catholic cemetery. Though, in 1814 he did have to file bankruptcy papers, he was laid to rest four years later in St. Charles Borromero Roman Catholic Cemetery.

YORK

YORK, THE SLAVE OF William Clark of the famous Lewis and Clark expedition became an ambassador of good will to foreign nations. As a slave he was pleased to share this great adventure in the wilderness and was busy developing some striking frontier skills, learning new Native languages and making friends among the strange people he met. Ambassador of good will he became, and a vital asset to the famous exploration of the Louisana Territory.

York was born around 1780 to house slaves of the Clark family in Virginia and grew up as the special friend of their son William, York's age. Slaveowning families sometimes encouraged their sons to take a good friend from among their slaves to share their youthful adventures. Each young man just had to remember clearly what his station in life was. In 1799 Clark inherited the family estate, and this included ownership of his childhood companion, York.

The two men were twenty-three when President Thomas Jefferson purchased Louisiana from Napoleon. Since no one knew what lay in this vast land that stretched from the Mississippi to the Pacific, the president asked his secretary Meriwether Lewis to lead an exploring party. Lewis promptly chose his friend Clark, and Clark just as quickly decided to bring along York. By this time York was an imposing man, six feet in height and weighing over two hundred pounds—in an age when most men were under five foot six.

In St. Louis, where the expedition trained for the trip, York began to pick up French and Indian words. By the time the task force set out, he was able to assist Sacagewea, the Shoshone woman, in translations. For the next two and a half years, the two dark explorers were able to convince one Native American Nation after another that the forty-three men and one woman came in peace.

York also became one of the party's best hunters, fishermen, and scouts. By the last year of the journey he was given the assignment of trading with the Indians for the expedition's food.

York was able to use more than his considerable frontier skills, command of language, and smiling good will. He was incredibly fast on his feet and utilized his agility and exotic looks when negotiating. Many Native Americans had never seen an African American before, certainly none of his size and strength. Clark's diary recorded how the Arikara "all flocked around him and examined him from top to toe." York responded to this attention by showing "his powers of strength" and telling the astonished Arikara that he had once been a "wild animal." His leaping agility won new friends for the expedition.

All the way to the Pacific coast, Clark wrote, Indian women

Artist Charles Russell painted this picture of York meeting the Mandan Indians in the northwest.

were "very fond" of York. Like other members of the force, York took Indian "wives" in the various villages they visited.

Among the Mandan Indians on the Upper Missouri, York leaped and danced his way into hearts, startling people that so "large a man should be so active" and agile. Fascinated by their black visitor, some Mandan villagers decided to rub York's black skin with a wet finger to see if the color would come off. Artist Charles M. Russell captured the moment in a famous painting.

More than the bright trinkets the explorers had brought to gain Indian attention, Shoshone, Nez Percé, and other nations along the Columbia River found York fascinating. York turned this fascination into a bargaining tool and became a skilled negotiator and diplomat.

By the end of 1805, Sacagewea and York had earned an equal voice in the expedition and were asked to vote with the others on the location of a winter camp. York had leaped far from slavery in Virginia.

One Flathead Indian tried to explain how his people saw York: "Those who had been brave and fearless, the victorious ones in battle, painted themselves in charcoal. So the black man, they thought, had been the bravest in the party."

Upon the expedition's return to St. Louis, everyone packed up and headed for home. Clark brought his slave back to Kentucky and dull routine. When Clark was appointed Governor of the Missouri Territory and Director of Indian Affairs, York went with him. He hired out near Louisville so he could be near his wife, who worked for a white family.

Clark eventually liberated York and gave him a wagon and six horses. With these he ran a transportation business between Nashville and Richmond. But the explorer saw his business go from bad to worse, and York eventually died of cholera.

Perhaps when one is lifted from slave life in Virginia to hack a unique path through the wilderness, the rest of life seems very dull. When one creates an original brand of frontier negotiation and deals effectively with Native Americans for an expedition authorized by President Jefferson, running a team of horses hardly compares.

THEIR MIXING IS TO BE PREVENTED

In Latin America, Africans had found safe places to hide and many Indians to aid them. Europeans were reluctant to seek out these remote hideouts. In North America, Africans were not that lucky.

To begin with, there were fewer Indians. The largest body of Native Americans east of the Mississippi, the Iroquois Confederacy, never numbered more than sixteen thousand men, women, and children. There were no rugged mountains, impenetrable jungles, and few hidden havens for runaways. Slaves who ran to the forests and hills found fewer red hands of friendship, and little military support. Daring fugitives could reach Indians in the backwoods, but so too could slavehunters and their tracking dogs.

BRITISH AMERICA

ON BOTH NORTHERN AND southern American continents, Europeans enslaved Africans and Native Americans to pile up profits in the shortest possible time. This led to laws and policies that were genocidal toward Indians and just short of that for Africans. In North America, the British added a new element to their relationship with people of color. It was a curious, sharp feeling of personal contempt—today we call it "racism." It often seemed as important for the English to emphasize the "inferiority" of dark people as it was to make a profit.

British merchants, missionaries, and soldiers quickly penetrated Native American villages with their beliefs and businesslike approach to life. By 1670 Indian men were using axes and hoes, wearing hats, shoes, stockings, breeches, and linen shirts, and carrying hatchets and knives made in England. Native women were using jewelry, brass kettles, thread, needles, scissors, petticoats, calico, lace, and mirrors produced across the Atlantic. Native Americans fought enemies with flints, muskets, powder, and bullets purchased from European merchants. They had become dependent on their white foes.

An erosion of native culture followed. People who worshiped nature began to practice the Christian religion of their enemies. Those who cared little for private gain and practiced cooperation in economic life were taught "everything has a price." From the first exchange of trinkets for land, muskets for corn, and Christianity for a native faith in nature, an entire culture was guided toward a European love of possession.

Since labor was in short supply in British America, the earliest colonists enslaved first Indians and then Africans. Since unending bondage did not exist in English law, the first form was called "indenture" and lasted for about seven years. "Indentured servants" of any color could be mistreated while in service, have their personal life regulated, and their time extended by scheming masters.

Since all three races were abused under this system, they often rebelled and escaped. Reward notices of the time tell of red, black, and white men and women fleeing their masters—sometimes together.

The first Africans introduced into Jamestown's economy in 1619 became indentured servants, not slaves. Upon their release, they became part of the Virginia colony. Some became landowners, and one, Anthony Johnson, ruled an African community of twelve homesteads and two hundred acres in Virginia's Northampton County.

In the 1630s the rules of indenture began to change. It became legal to hold Africans or Indians for more than the usual seven years, even for life. The change began on the English-ruled island of Barbados when the governor announced "that Negroes and Indians . . . should serve for life, unless a contract was made to the contrary." And beginning in 1636, only whites received contracts of indenture.

British America had taken a large step in dividing labor by race and reserving the worst for people of color. More and more white laborers were pouring into the thirteen British colonies, and masters did not want them making common cause with Africans or Native Americans. Masters had probably concluded their profitable labor system would work only as long as whites did not see their condition and fate as tied to people of color.

In 1636 a Massachusetts Indian became the first North American to be legally enslaved, sentenced to work until he died. A decade later Governor John Winthrop thought of the idea of seizing Narragansett Indians to exchange for Africans. Around the same time British commissioners meeting in New Haven also decided that it was fair to make slaves of Indians and exchange them for Africans.

By 1661 slavery had become legal in the British colonies. Africans were preferred since they were thousands of miles from home. Indian slaves were able to flee to their armed brothers and sisters—and then come roaring back armed and revengeful.

This idea of keeping slaves distant from their homes and families was crucial to having them under strict control. British merchants took Indians enslaved on the mainland and shipped them to the West Indies. This was the only safe way to enslave Native Americans, for bondage was only secure when its victims had no one to turn to, no family or friends nearby.

Reward notices in colonial newspapers now told of African slaves who "ran off with his Indian wife" or "had kin among the Indians" or is "part-Indian and speaks their language good."

In slave huts and beyond the British settlements along the coast, African and Native American women and men shared their sorrows and hopes, their luck and courage. They did not always know where to run to, but they knew where to run from.

Judging from reward notices, Africans picked up Indian languages as soon as they reached a frontier region. Runaways in the woods always needed outside help.

The first full-scale battle between Native Americans and British colonists took place in Jamestown, Virginia, in 1622. Africans fared a lot better than their owners. According to historian James H. Johnstone "the Indians murdered every white but saved the Negroes." This, noted Johnstone, became a common pattern during wars between colonists and Indians.

British colonial law not only lumped Native American and African people together, but handed both worse punishments than whites. A Virginia law set twenty-five lashes for whites who stole pigs, but increased this to thirty-nine lashes if the accused were a red or black person. Virginia soon declared "Negro, Mulatto and Indian slaves . . . to be real estate."

Beginning slowly in 1670, rules of bondage began to change to permit Native Americans to leave. Virginia began matters that year by stating that Indians were enslaved for only twelve years, Africans for life.

This decision was based on a peculiar legal point that Africans were "imported into this colony by shipping" and Indians came "by land." No mention was made of the fact that Indians did not come by land, but had lived there before English settlers arrived, or that most Africans had been living in Virginia for much longer than most British citizens.

Before Indians were eased out of the slave system, they had lived and married with African slaves, and produced in their offspring a new class of Americans held in chains. When the slave codes talked of "Indian slaves," it probably meant those Black Indians. For example, although New York's Assembly banned Indian bondage in 1679, in 1682 it forbad "Negro or Indian Slaves" from leaving their masters' homes or plantations without permission. The next year the Assembly denied "Negro or Indian Slaves" from meeting anywhere together in groups of four or more or being armed "with guns, Swords, Clubs, Staves or Any Other kind of weapon."

Between 1619 and 1700 labor in North America had become divided by skin color. Liberty itself would remain divisible by skin color through the American Revolution and up to the Civil War and emancipation.

This division kept working people in America from uniting

against an unjust labor system. Masters deported Indian slaves to the West Indies so they could not flee to their homes and loved ones. They enlisted whites and local Indians to help them hunt their runaway African slaves. When local Native Americans refused this work, they reached out to Indians on distant islands who needed money or trade. Through this cleverness, slaveowners hoped to sleep soundly each night and awake each day to greater profits.

THE SOUTHERN FRONTIER

TO AN EXTENT RARELY revealed in Hollywood frontier movies, slave labor built the earliest European communities in the south. From 1690 to 1720, Africans cleared land, introduced African rice culture, navigated river vessels, and delivered the mail in the Carolinas. Only the most trustworthy slaves were brought to the frontier, and most stood by their masters. But some fled to the woods and Indians at the first opportunity, giving their owners something more to worry about.

For British subjects the question of bringing slaves so close to the frontier and Native Americans stirred a lively debate. A South Carolina law of 1725 imposed a £200 fine on those who brought their slaves to the frontier. A British colonel urged enforcement "because the Slaves . . . talk good English as well as the Cherokee language and . . . too often tell falsities to the Indians which they are apt to believe." In 1751, another law warned "The carrying of Negroes among the Indians has all along been thought detrimental, as an intimacy ought to be avoided."

But sound racial policies on the frontier clashed with the

George Washington and his surveying team, which included an African American

desire to reap the profits produced by slave labor. Virginia surveyor George Washington, twenty-three, urged the use of "mulattoes and Negroes . . . as pioneers and hatchet men" in the wilderness. An early print shows a young Washington with a black-and-white surveying team.

British colonists tried to play one dark race against the other on the southern frontier. The Maryland Assembly in 1676 offered Indians rewards for recapturing slave runaways. In South Carolina, in 1708, 5,280 European settlers tried to watch over 2,900 African and 1,400 Indian slaves. Europeans sent slave "cattle hunters" to protect Charleston from Indians.

The conflict among the three races on the frontier had each side seeking allies wherever they could be found. During the Yemassee War of 1715, Natchez Indians murdered whites and seized their slaves. When the British ordered one thousand two hundred soldiers against the Natchez, they sent black troops along. And when Governor Charles Craven of South Carolina confronted the Natchez's army he found it also included armed black prisoners.

By 1739 the frontier racial cauldron was boiling over in South Carolina and Louisiana. Slaves rose in rebellion at Stono, South Carolina. Terrified whites turned to Catawbas Indians, noted for their slavehunting skills, to recapture or slay all rebels. In Louisiana, the governor was shocked to learn Chickasaws had contacted a daring band of Banbara Africans enslaved at New Orleans. His spies told him the two peoples plotted an insurrection that would kill whites and create a red-black maroon confederacy.

Hardly had he solved this threat when he heard New Orleans was menaced by Chouchas Indians a few miles north. The governor sent off armed black slaves to carry out a massacre.

These sporadic conflicts hardly matched the unending racial disturbances along the border between British Georgia and Spanish Florida. Spain relied largely on the Africans and Indians of Florida to resist any invasion by slavehunting British. When Georgia Governor Oglethorpe invaded Florida in 1740, Spain's red and black troops repelled him. Oglethorpe learned that two hundred Africans, including many ex-slaves from Georgia, guarded St. Augustine.

When Spain ordered a counterattack on Georgia in 1742, their armed forces included a black regiment and "negro commanders clothed in lace" bearing the same rank as white officers. The British concluded they had more to worry about from this force starting a slave revolt in Georgia than from anything Spanish troops might do.

Throughout this time, no figure in Florida terrified the British more than Francisco Menendez, a swashbuckling African who fought alongside the Yamasee Indians for ten years. The acknowledged leader of the many runaways who accepted Spain's offer to exchange bondage under the British for freedom in Florida, Menendez became a skilled military commander. In 1738, Menendez petitioned the Spanish to found Gracia Real de Santa Teresa de Mose as a separate town for his people and as a walled fortress that would guard St. Augustine two miles away. Fort Mose's one hundred men and women of color were more than an armed community living in huts resembling an Indian village. They formed North America's first officially free African American and Black Indian community.

The British first tasted Fort Mose's power in 1739 when sixty enslaved men and women rose in Stono, South Carolina—southwest of Charleston, North Carolina—and killed twenty whites and then headed south toward Fort Mose. This largest armed strike for liberty in North America was surrounded by British militiamen and massacred.

The next year, Georgia's British governor Oglethorpe marched his army on St. Augustine, and forced Menendez to evacuate Fort Mose. But Menendez then marshaled his African and Native

Americans forces, threw back Oglethorpe's soldiers, and regained his fort.

But in 1763 the British claimed Florida, and Spain helped relocate these Black Indian families to Cuba and to freedom.

At around this time British colonists in the southern colonies began introducing the practice of African slavery among neighboring Native Americans. They concentrated on the Five Nations—Cherokees, Chickasaws, Choctaws, Creeks, and Seminoles—as the largest body of Indians present on their borders. Their aim was to make their slave property more secure by making Indians partners in the system. Indians who accepted slavery, they reasoned, would not take in fleeing runaways.

Except for the Seminoles, the Five Nations began to accept the foreign idea of slavery. Even so, their idea of how it should

This early twentieth-century photograph of a Cherokee mother sitting with her daughter indicates the child's father was probably of African descent.

work differed from British practices. Quaker slaveholder John Bartram, botanist to the king of England, visited some Indian owners in 1770. He found their slaves dressed better than the chief, married into the nation easily, and their children were "free, and considered in every respect equal" to other members. After a visit to the Creeks, Bartram wrote:

> I saw in every town in the Nation I visited captives, some extremely aged, who were free and in as good circumstances as their masters; and all slaves have their freedom when they marry, which is permitted and encouraged [and] they and their offspring are in every way upon an equality with their conquerers.

But how did Native Americans view the way Europeans treated their enslaved Africans? Two European missionaries, trying to convert the Delaware Nation, returned rejected but with this report on the Delaware response to their plea:

> They rejoiced exceedingly at our happiness in thus being favored by the Great Spirit, and felt very grateful that we had condescended to remember our brethren in the wilderness. But they could not help recollecting that we had a people among us, whom, because they differed from us in color, we had made slaves of, and made them suffer great hardships, and lead miserable lives. Now they could not see any reason, if a people being black entitled us then to deal with them, why a red color should not equally qualify the same treatment.

They therefore had determined to wait, to see whether all the black people amongst us were made thus happy and joyful before they would put confidence in our promises; for they thought a people who had suffered so much and so long by our means, should be entitled to our first attention; and therefore they had sent back the two missionaries, with many thanks, promising that when they saw the black people among us restored to freedom and happiness they would gladly receive our missionaries.

Despite every European effort to keep one people of color from assisting the other, the two races began to blend on a vast scale. Black Indians were apparent everywhere if one bothered to look. Thomas Jefferson, for example, found among the Mattaponies of his Virginia, "more negro than Indian blood in them." Another eyewitness reported Virginia's Gingaskin reservation had become "largely African." Peter Kalm, whose famous diary described a visit to the British colonies in 1750, took note of many Africans living with Indians, with marriage and children the normal result.

That same year a Moravian missionary, J. C. Pyrlaeus, visited the Nanticoke Nation on Maryland's eastern shore to compile a vocabulary of their language. Years later, their words were discovered to form a language that was pure African Mandingo.

British authorities repeatedly tried to convince Native Americans to return the slave fugitives they harbored in their villages. But here they collided with an Indian adoption system that welcomed new members and offered them full protection. When whites argued about the right of private property in owning people and insisted Africans were inferior beings, the Indians shrugged "no."

In treaty after treaty southern colonists made native nations promise to return fugitive slaves. In 1721, the Five Nations solemnly promised a governor of Virginia to deliver slaves, but nothing happened. The British complained bitterly on behalf of their slave owners, the chiefs apologized, and the ex-slaves became a part of Native American life.

When angry slavehunters decided to take matters into their own hands, they met fierce opposition. In 1750 Captain Tobias Fitch sent off a posse of five to retrieve a slave living in the Creek Nation. A Creek chief stood between them and the black man, cut their rope and threw it in a fire. Then he warned them his villagers had as many guns as they did. The posse returned empty-handed and happy to be alive.

African members of the Indian Nation often played a vital part in armed resistance to whites. In 1727 Africans and Indians besieged Virginia frontier settlements. During the French and Indian War a British officer, warning about the two races, said "Their mixing is to be prevented as much as possible."

THE NORTHERN BRITISH COLONIES

IN THE NEW ENGLAND and Middle Colonies African slaves were less numerous and therefore considered less dangerous. But in their actions and laws, whites in these colonies showed a fear that people of color would unite against them.

This sketch of an early Rhode Island school for Native American and African American children had a teacher who was also a woman of color.

In 1690 a Connecticut law forbad red or black people from walking beyond town limits without a pass. Ferrymen were warned not to take people of either race across rivers. Connecticut, Rhode Island, and Massachusetts had laws imposing a nine o'clock curfew on Africans and Native Americans. Other New England laws were aimed at people of color who broke streetlights, sold liquor, met together at night, or were entertained by Europeans.

Some laws specifically sought to prevent insurrections. In 1773 New York's Common Council in Albany passed a curfew "to prevent Negro and Indian slaves from appearing in the streets after eight at night without a lantern with a lighted candle in it."

They could not remain in Boston Common after sunset and were not allowed to carry a cane or stick "or anything else that could be fit for quarreling or fighting." Rhode Island, with the largest African population in New England, banned their outdoor social gatherings.

These laws may have complicated and slowed, but failed to halt associations between the two peoples. So many slaves fled to the Six Nations of the Iroquois Confederacy that, in 1726, a governor of New York made the leading chiefs promise to return all fugitives in their villages. They gave their word. In 1764 Hurons also promised. The next year Delawares promised. None ever returned a single slave.

There are many instances, however, when the two peoples of color acted in concert and terrified New England colonists. In 1660 African and Native American raiders panicked Hartford, Connecticut, residents with an armed night assault. In 1690 Isaac Morill, British, James Dole, African, and Joseph Moody, Indian, were arrested in Newbury, Connecticut, for a major conspiracy against the state. Morill admitted helping foment a rebellion with the French that would arm Africans so "that the English would be cut off." Morrill and his confederates planned to lead a French and Indian force from Canada that would "save none but the Indians and Negroes."

These startling revelations sent many colonists to bed each night frightened lest this combination of foes might prevent the dawn. Half a century later, in 1738, Nantucket, Rhode Island, residents uncovered an Indian plot to attack their city at night and only spare Africans.

Near Ontario, British colonists worried about activities on Chief Joseph Brant's Mohawk reservation. Although Brant was loyal to British interests, he welcomed slave runaways to his nation and may have encouraged intermarriage with his Mohawks.

During Chief Pontiac's uprising against the British, Brant and his Mohawks stood solidly by their British allies. But around Detroit, reported a white resident, "the Indians are saving and caressing all the Negroes they take." He was very worried lest this might "produce an insurrection."

With few Indians or Africans in the northern colonies, there were fewer opportunities for the two peoples to meet or plot. And there were fewer Black Indians compared to what had become common in Virginia and the southern colonies at this time. These factors, and the relatively mild treatment of slaves by northern masters, made slaves less willing to risk their lives by fleeing or planning rebellions.

It was not uncommon for New England slaves to view Indians much as their masters did and to side with whites during Indian warfare. In 1746 Lucy Terry, sixteen and African-born, witnessed a battle between Indians and her white neighbors in Deerfield, Massachusetts. Her rhymed story of it, "The Bar's Fight," described whites as valiant, brave, and bold and called Indians heartless murderers.

This poem became the first published by an African in the New World and made Terry a celebrity, much in demand to recite her verses before local audiences.

From that point, Lucy Terry had no trouble with Native Americans. The same cannot be said about her relations with her white neighbors. She married an ex-slave, Elijah Prince, and two of their sons served in George Washington's Army. But the Princes were not destined to enjoy "the rights of man" promised by the patriot victory. Their prosperous farm was hit by a series of fires set by a neighbor who wanted the land. Haystacks were set afire and fences torn down at night. Through her determined plea before the governor, Lucy Prince won a cease and desist order.

When Mrs. Prince tried to enroll her youngest son in Williams College, she was told blacks were not welcome. She argued eloquently with the trustees, pointing to her family's military record, citing the Bible and the Declaration of Independence, but to no avail. When she died at ninety-one, in 1821, the Massachusetts legislature had established a committee to determine if the state could expel any black person who entered.

Perhaps the Lucy Terry Prince experience meant that a black person had less to fear from an Indian on the warpath than from a white man with a pen or plow.

By the end of the colonial period in British America, bondage had been confined to Africans, their children, and those Black Indians caught in the European web. Each century, great Native American figures arose to call on Indians of every nation to combine against the European invaders. There was King Philip in the 1670s, Pontiac in the 1760s, and Tecumseh in the 1810s. None understood that their best potential allies slept each night, a stone's throw of the enemy.

LIKE THE INDIANS THEMSELVES

GRIZZLED, UNCOUTH, AND UNWASHED, the old fur trappers looked more like the mountain bears they claimed they could wrestle than like men. They earned their place in history and talked their way into American folklore, and for good reason. They spun the tallest tales, especially to exaggerate their strength and accomplishments. But they also discovered more US rivers and mountain passes than all the government expeditions sent out for that purpose.

But most incredibly, they rolled up this astounding record while seeking furs and pelts from Indians who sold them and hacking their way back to their European customers.

Each day these frontiersmen faced mysterious perils. A snap of a twig, a screech from an unfamiliar bird, or the snarl of a ferocious animal might announce a brush with death. Sometimes there was no announcement. Trappers had to train eyes, ears, and nose to detect friend or foe—and to speedily note the difference.

Their business drove them ever westward, seeking remote Native Americans less likely to know the great value Europeans placed on furs or skins. By 1850 their frontier daring had taken hunting and transformed it into a major US industry.

The fur industry's business methods left a lot to be desired. General Zachary Taylor once characterized agents of John Jacob Astor's huge American Fur Company as "the greatest scoundrels the world ever knew."

Hollywood stereotyped the fur trappers as men from either Scotland or France. With names like McBayne or Roget, Beaufont or MacIntosh—and accents to match the names—white trappers strode across our silver screens. None ever looked like Edward Rose, James Beckwourth, or George and Pierre Bonga.

In reality, however, African Americans were among the trade's leading figures—as entrepreneurs, voyageurs, and hunters. Colonel James Stevenson of the Bureau of American Ethnology spent thirty years living among and studying Native Americans. In 1888 he wrote: ". . . the old fur traders always got a Negro if possible to negotiate for them with the Indians, because of their 'pacifying effect.' They could manage them better than the white men, with less friction."

Trading with Indians mixed diplomacy with business, and that Native Americans preferred blacks to Europeans is hardly surprising given the European record of conquest.

Beginning in 1673, when fur trader Louis Joliet and Father Jacques Marquette used five African voyageurs to paddle their canoes down the Mississippi to the mouth of the Arkansas, black men were a vital part of fur-trapping expeditions.

There is a problem in reconstructing the lives of black trappers because white scholars have often doubted their honesty.

The tall tale has always been a part of frontier Americana, but black frontiersmen have been accused of so distorting their personal stories as to blot out the truth.

James Beckwourth, for example, has long been considered, in the words of one professor, "rather as a great liar than as a great 'mountain man.'" In 1848 General William Tecumseh Sherman met Beckwourth and wrote this contradictory judgment: "Jim Beckwourth . . . was in my estimate, one of the best chroniclers of events on the plains that I have ever encountered, though his reputation for veracity was not good." For two pages of his book the famous General described how a Beckwourth story, though doubted, led to the capture of four murderers sought by the US Army.

Some frontier historians have admitted linking truthfulness to race. Historian Frances Parkman scribbled in his personal copy of Beckwourth's autobiography "Much of this narrative is probably false" and added "Beckwourth is a fellow of bad character—a compound of white and black blood." A more modern scholar has written that black frontiersman Edward Rose was "a morose, moody misfit of mixed blood and lawless disposition." Once blood is made the measure of a person, it is the one who measures, not the historical figure, who creates a distortion.

The evidence on Rose and Beckwourth shows that they commanded high wages, were much in demand by fur companies, and trusted by Native Americans. Frontier businessmen or Native Americans were not likely to heap rewards on chronic liars or men who could not be trusted with valuables or other humans.

>| |<

THE BIG NEWS BROUGHT back by the Lewis and Clark expedition was that the huge Louisiana Territory was filled with valuable fur animals and friendly Indians. The Missouri River offered an all-water route to these rich hunting grounds.

Of the fur-trading expeditions assembling in the winter of 1806–1807 at St. Louis, Manuel Lisa's proved the most important. Into its ranks stepped Edward Rose, until that moment a man of unknown accomplishments. Perhaps he was too young or inexperienced to have achieved a record at this date. Not even that is known.

The Lisa foray into the wilderness would forever establish Rose's reputation as one of the North American continent's leading frontiersmen, one sensitive to the task of dealing with Native Americans. The Lisa band sailed up the Missouri and Yellowstone rivers by keelboat and then built Fort Manuel at the mouth of the Big Horn. The men spent the next year's winter trapping, trading with natives, and fanning out from their camps to find more furs.

The Manuel Lisa expedition returned with the valuable news that greatest profits would go to large companies rather than individual traders. This information transformed the fur trade from a small operation into a company effort and a big business. Rose became one of the experts able to explain the best ways to operate in the wilderness.

He soon became a guide, hunter, and interpreter for the Missouri Fur Company, the Rocky Mountain Fur Company of William Ashley, and the American Fur Company of John Jacob Astor. Rose established a tradition of friendship between his white friends and the Native Americans they encountered.

Contemporaries described Rose as awesome. Thickset, muscular, above average in height, he had a slash on his nose, a scar on his forehead, and a grim, serious look. He meant business. No one knew if his slashed nose was a result of a fight or an accident; Indians called him "Cut-Nose." Rose came from ancestors that included Cherokees, Africans, and Europeans. He knew a dozen Native American languages and Indian sign language.

Those who knew him well described Rose as strong, daring, and sometimes reckless, a man whose exploits matched anything in fiction. Washington Irving wrote of Rose in his *Astoria* and in the *Adventures of Captain Bonneville*, calling him "powerful in frame and fearless in spirit." Another author said Rose's "incredible career makes the most adventurous fiction seem weak and pallid."

Rose was ever on the move and always found his skills in demand. In 1809, he ventured with Ezekial Williams to the Yellowstone, the first land expedition into its beaver country. During the journey Rose proved capable of the sensitive task of guarding Mandan Chief Big White all the way back to his home. In 1811 Rose served as interpreter and guide for Wilson B. Hunt when he led Astor's men to western lands. The next year Rose was paid $250 for a one-month trip of five hundred miles to the Crow Nation. When measured against the $250 yearly wage paid other trappers at the time, his pay was very high.

Rose, who became a Crow chief at one point in his career, lived among various Native Americans for years, understood their languages and developed trusting relationships. This came in handy. According to one report, when General Ashley's party was attacked by Native Americans, some of the attackers called out to Rose "to take care of himself, before they fired on General Ashley's party."

What exactly did he do to get along well with Native Americans? In his 1848 book, *Five Scalps,* Captain Reuben Holmes describes Rose's qualities "that gained him the respect of the Indians" in these words:

> He was as cunning as a prairie wolf. He was a perfect woodsman. He could endure any kind of fatigue and privation as well as the best trained Indians. He studied men. There was nothing that an Indian could do, that Rose did not make himself master of. He knew all that Indians knew. He was a great man in his situation.

Rose, as much as Beckwourth and most trappers and frontiersmen, loved and told a good tale. It mixed fact with that personal brand of self-puffery known as the tall story. A recognized, imitated, and enjoyable form of frontier humor, it began with Captain John Smith and Daniel Boone and still rides high with hunters and fishermen.

Rose and Beckwourth did expand a truth when it touched on their skills and accomplishments. They also let the flow of events and the efforts of others unfold undisturbed.

GEORGE AND STEPHEN BONGA

COMPARED WITH THE EXPLOSIVE life of Edward Rose, the for the American Fur Company, maintaining posts at La Platte, businesslike fur-trapping experiences of the Bonga brothers seem as quiet as a frozen Minnesota lake. However, this frontier Black Chippewa family negotiated some key Indian treaties for the US government and built some important Minnesota trading outposts.

The first Bongas to arrive in Minnesota were a slave couple brought there by a British officer after the American Revolution. They had a son Pierre, who was apprenticed to a Canadian trapper for the North West Company and was well trusted. Together with a white man, he was put in charge of the company fort when his master left on business. In time Pierre Bonga became an interpreter for the North West Company. While negotiating in a Chippewa village he met and fell in love with a Chippewa woman, and they were married.

Pierre Bonga and his bride settled in Duluth half a century before a permanent European settlement was established there. During the presidency of Thomas Jefferson their son George was born, and his father was able to send him to school in Montreal. When he returned home, George also chose a Chippewa woman as his bride. George and his brother Stephen followed in their father's footsteps, becoming fur trappers, learning French and English, Chippewa, and other Indian languages.

George Bonga cultivated a close relationship with the twenty-five thousand-strong Chippewa Nation at a critical time for the US government. In 1837, at Fort Snelling, George Bonga was able to negotiate a key treaty between his country and his people for Governor Lewis Cass of the Michigan Territory. Cass later became a presidential candidate and liked to tell of his part in this historic transaction.

In his work as a trapper, George Bonga served as a voyageur

George Bonga

for the American Fur Company, maintaining posts at La Platte, Otter Tail Lake, and Leech Lake, where he made his home.

The Bonga brothers were tall, powerfully built, ebony-black

men. They were known in Minnesota for their gentle ways, quick humor, love of storytelling, and hospitality.

In 1856, as the slavery controversy exploded into border warfare in Kansas, George Bonga and his wife entertained a distinguished guest. Judge Charles Flandreau, after an exhausting canoe trip to the source of the Mississippi, came to their cabin and was invited to stay for two weeks.

George Bonga, whom Flandreau described as "the blackest man I ever saw," regaled his guests with tales of old trapping experiences. Everyone enjoyed a laugh when Bonga said, "Gentlemen, I assure you that John Banfil and myself were the first two white men that ever came to this country."

To amuse his guest, Bonga assembled a crew for an early day's lake voyage, complete with "a splendid birch bark canoe," manned by twelve hearty men. Led by Bonga and "to the music of a French Canadian," the judge learned "how royally they travelled" when Minnesota was wild country.

Some forty-two years later, then associate justice of the Minnesota Supreme Court, Flandreau wrote of his vacation with "this thorough gentleman" and "prominent trader and man of wealth and consequence." It is the only account of George Bonga's personal side.

The next year the Bongas entertained two traders at their Otter Tail Lake post. This time the Black Chippewa eagerly asked "about elections and political matters." The United States was hurtling toward Civil War and black people had a vital stake in the day's political questions.

The Bonga family bequeathed the state of Minnesota about a hundred descendants and gave their name to Bonga township in Cass County.

*This 1899 photograph of Native American fur trappers in Minnesota also
includes two members of the Bonga family (far right; far left, back row).*

JAMES P. BECKWOURTH

BLACK TRAPPERS TRIED MIGHTILY to build bridges of
understanding with Native Americans, sometimes cemented
with bonds of marriage. James Beckwourth also married Indian
women, sometimes in dizzyingly rapid succession. But with his
flaming temper and love of battle he kept burning his bridges.

Beckwourth became a chieftain of both Crow and Blackfoot
Indian Nations, so he enjoyed many supporters and admirers.
Beckwourth also emerges from the fur trade's early history as
"the greatest Indian fighter of his generation." This was an age
when his competitors for this "honor" were Daniel Boone, Davy

Van Heflin (right); Jim Bridger; and Jack Oakie (left), as Jim Beckwourth, in the 1951 Technicolor Hollywood classic Tomahawk.

Crockett, Jim Bridger, and Kit Carson.

It is difficult to imagine that this famed frontiersman, scout, and explorer has faded from the story of the Old West, but fade he did. In skill, accomplishment, and violence, he matched men whose deeds have become part of a "glorious frontier heritage." But when Universal International in Hollywood produced the horse opera *Tomahawk* in 1951, it cast white actor Jack Oakie as Jim Beckwourth. Generations of young people never learned that this tough pioneer fur trapper was a black man with Native American ancestry.

Beckwourth was born around 1798 to a black slave with Native American lineage, and her white master. As a teenager, he was apprenticed to a St. Louis blacksmith. His western adventures began with a punch. When the burly blacksmith came between Beckwourth and his liberty at nineteen to come and go as he pleased, Beckwourth slugged him and left St. Louis for the wilderness. Though hardly original, he had "hit" upon the solution to problems he would use from there on.

In a business that moved as fast as foot, boat, or horse could carry it, Beckwourth swept from one end of the continent to the other, from St. Louis to Salt Lake, from California to Florida, from New Orleans to Nevada. On the trail he fought or made friends with Native American Blackfeet, Sac, Snakes, and Crows.

His Indian wives invariably were royalty, daughters of chiefs who could do Beckwourth some good. No woman ever held him for very long, and one Blackfoot chief's daughter was almost killed by Beckwourth on their wedding night. When she refused to obey his command not to dance, he clobbered her with the side of an axe. Turning to her father, he explained that discipline had to be maintained.

The chief not only agreed, but gave him a new daughter. That night Beckwourth and his second wife of the day were spending their honeymoon in a teepee when the first wife came crawling back. Beckwourth settled the issue by giving both women presents and then taking his leave.

In a Crow village, Beckwourth was adopted into the nation and married the chief's daughter. First named "Morning Star," after leading Crows into battle, he was renamed "Bloody Arm." He soon found life among the Crows too quiet and left for new excitement.

In the 1830s he served as a US Army scout in the Seminole wars—against the Black Seminole alliance in Florida. Enemies were enemies and a good fight, after all, was a good fight. In 1843 Pathfinder John C. Frémont met Beckwourth traveling with a Spanish wife sixty miles east of the Rockies. Another time Beckworth met General Kearny during California's Bear Flag Rebellion. Kearny told him "You like war, and I have good use for you now."

Later Beckwourth prospected for gold, trapped some more, and wandered. By then he carried such Indian names as Bull's Robe, Medicine Calf, and White-Handled Knife. He dressed, looked, and acted like a Native American. When he became a Crow

James P. Beckwourth

chief, he led his men into battle stripped down and shouting, "I will show you how to fight."

In April 1850, Beckwourth made a discovery that should have forever earned him a place in US history books. Northwest of what is now Reno, Nevada, and on what is now Route 70 in California, he found a pass through the Sierra Nevada mountains. It soon became an important gateway to Gold Rush California.

Today the pass, mountain peak, and town nearby still bear Beckwourth's name. He personally led the first wagon train through Beckwourth Pass. Later he built a hotel and retired to become a peaceful innkeeper.

In 1855 Beckwourth met journalist T. D. Bonner in San Francisco and the two began to collaborate on *The Life and*

Adventures of James P. Beckwourth. Beckwourth talked and Bonner wrote and the resulting volume appeared the next year. It is silent on the matter of Beckwourth's dark ancestors, and its artist's sketches make him appear white.

In November 1864, Jim Beckwourth, at sixty-nine, suffered from rheumatism and poor eyesight, and was proud of decades of good relations with Native Americans. Then Colorado militia colonel John Chivington and nine hundred of his volunteers rode up to recruit him for an attack on a peaceful Arapaho and Cheyenne village at Sand Creek, where Black Kettle had been promised army protection. Chivington wanted Beckwourth to help him "collect scalps and wade in blood." Beckwourth said no, but Chivington threatened to hang him, and the old scout saddled up.

At dawn Chivington's army reached Sand Creek, where Black Kettle's six hundred people—mostly women and children—gathered under a large American flag. Black Kettle raised a white flag and told everyone to "not be afraid."

Beckwourth stared with horror as Chivington's men began to fire wildly with four howitzers and rifles. He saw people shot dead as they held up their hands. Then men charged in to finish the job with pistols, swords, and knives. "There seemed to be indiscriminate slaughter of men, women and children. . . . I saw quite a number of mothers were slain; still clinging to their babies," reported another Indian scout. A white lieutenant, James Connor, described children and babies butchered or mutilated with swords and left to die while others were scalped. Hundreds died before the day was over.

Fearing war, US officials sent Beckwourth to negotiate with Chief Leg in the Water and his council. Acts of retaliation would only bring overwhelming white force, Beckwourth pleaded. The council answered: "But what do we want to live for? The white man has taken our country, killed all our game . . . killed our wives and children. Now no peace." Colorado fell into its own civil war with brutality on both sides.

In 1866, Beckwourth died of food poisoning while traveling to or from a Crow village. This simple fact has given rise to a legend: He was invited back to his Crow people by those who hoped he would consent to lead them again. When Beckwourth refused, this legend continues, he was given a feast and poisoned. Unable to have him as a live chief, Crows would keep him forever in their burial grounds. This fantasy touches truth in the admiration his fellow Crows had for him, and in their profound sense of loss when he left them.

Beckwourth was part of that daring, brutal frontier tradition that opened the wilderness to white exploration and settlement. He was clearly a man suited to the dangers of the trail, one who fought and killed with ease and even pleasure. "Probably no man ever lived who has met with more personal adventure including danger to life," wrote his biographer, T. D. Bonner.

Even if this is an exaggeration, it indicates that Beckwourth belongs in the pages of our violent frontier epic as much as his better known contemporaries.

BLOOD SO LARGELY MINGLED

IN THE DECADES BEFORE the Civil War, frantic slaveholders tried to nail down and secure their leaky system. For seven cents an hour they hired armed patrols to scour the countryside every night. Savage beatings awaited any African American man, woman, or child walking without a pass. Runaways were tracked with savage dogs. Free blacks were carefully watched lest they give aid and comfort to fleeing sisters and brothers—which they often did. Antislavery whites were warned, tarred and feathered, or driven from their homes.

But there was one slave escape hatch that drove slaveowners to sputtering fury. Whites looked at Native American villages in the South and found black faces staring back at them. Paranoia told whites that these people were about to rise up, liberate slaves, and kill whites.

This haunting Black Indian presence spelled a trouble or doom that had to be dealt with. One hysterical response was to demand that state legislatures remove Indians from tax exempt lands, and then drive them away.

In 1843, for example, white residents of King William County, Virginia, felt their world was coming to an end—"unhinged" they said. As a slaveholding community they petitioned their legislature to save them from what they termed a "dangerous" and "deadly" peril. At any moment they anticipated an attack by land and sea.

Their great fear was prompted by a peaceful community of Pamunkey Indians, many of whom were biracial or free black men and women. Rather than clarify their dangerous actions or suspected conspiracies, whites just kept pointing to the fact they were Black Indians. "Not one individual can be found among them whose grandfathers or grandmothers one or more is not of Negro blood," read a petition to the legislature.

The other white complaint charged Pamunkeys had allowed their land to become a "resort of free Negroes from all parts of the country" and a "harbour for runaway slaves." No evidence was offered for either accusation. But whites asked Virginia's assembly to deny the Pamunkeys their tax exemption and investigate their subversion of Virginia.

The real meaning of this furor was that it had become clear to any who cared to look that Native Americans east of the Mississippi had become a biracial people (with a sprinkling of white blood). In slaveholding regions this prompted white panic, and in northern states it led to legislative investigations.

ALONG THE ATLANTIC COAST

SLAVEHOLDERS KNEW BETTER THAN anyone that almost anything might disrupt their slave system. The presence of

Indian communities on their borders that included African Americans spelled possible sabotage, subversion, and a haven for slave runaways.

Petitions against the Gingaskin reservation began to reach the Virginia legislature as early as 1783. Whites in Northampton County complained free blacks and "other disorderly persons" were hiding there. When this petition failed, they tried again three years later, and lost again.

They petitioned again in 1812. This time war fever was loose in the land, and in Florida armed Seminoles openly defied US troops and slavehunters. The Virginia legislature removed the Gingaskins' tax exemption, saying they were no longer "Indians."

The Melungeon Indians in Tennessee and North Carolina faced similar charges. Whites in Tennessee declared Melungeons "free persons of color," so they continued to accept and marry black people. But in 1855, North Carolina Melungeons were forbidden to marry black people. The state legislature decided that these Melungeons were really Croatans. Croatans were considered white descendants of Sir Walter Raleigh's lost English colony of Roanoke. The Melungeon's "race" shifted with white legal decisions in their home states.

In the decades between the American Revolution and the Civil War Black Indian societies were reported in New Jersey, New York, Delaware, Maryland, Virginia, North Carolina, South Carolina, Connecticut, Tennessee, and Massachusetts. Some managed to live as maroons, distant from a white society they rejected.

White citizens viewed these communities with feelings ranging from curiosity to suspicion and dread. They charged some with being a stain on the larger society. Others were accused of dangerous inbreeding. White men kept their wives and children

A Kiowa married couple, Etla (right) and Lone Wolf (left) posed for this Matthew Brady photograph.

away, and kept their powder dry.

Northern states were also worried enough by a Black Indian presence to send investigators. Rhode Island, Long Island, and New Jersey reported thorough mixtures of the two peoples. A report on the Narragansetts found they were "nearly all . . . of mixed blood and color, in various degrees and shades." The same was said in state reports on New York's Southhampton and Montauk Indians. A shocked legislature concluded "they are only Indian in name." New Jersey state investigators claimed their Native Americans had lost their "Indian features."

Nowhere was the blending of Native American and African people clearer than in Massachusetts. Pioneer black historian Carter G. Woodson discovered an 1861 report by the state senate that listed Black Indians among most Massachusetts Indians: Hassanamisco, Middleborough, Chappequiddick, Christiantown,

Gay Head, Marshpee, Herring Pond, Fall River, and Dudley. Turning from these files to interview people in 1919, Woodson found African American residents who could trace their ancestry back to the famous Massasoit.

WILDFIRE, OR EDMONIA LEWIS

PERHAPS THE MOST ARTISTICALLY talented Black Indian of these eastern nations was Wildfire or Edmonia Lewis, daughter of a Chippewa mother and an African American father. Only three when her mother died in 1849, she was left in the care of two Chippewa aunts.

She grew up in upstate New York making and selling moccasins, bead baskets, and pincushions. "Until I was twelve years old," she recalled, "I led this wandering life, fishing and swimming." During this time she was known by her Chippewa name of Wildfire.

From 1860 to 1862,

Black Indian artist Edmonia Lewis

with funds supplied by her brother, Sunrise, she attended Oberlin College. There she changed her name to Edmonia Lewis and began to show an interest in sculpture. In a terrifying turn of events, she was accused and tried for poisoning two white Oberlin friends. In a well-publicized trial, she won an acquittal. Even this bizarre intrusion did not keep her from pursuing her artistic interest. She did have a "thought of returning to the wild life again, but my love of sculpture forbade it."

Lewis left Oberlin for Boston, where she met prominent black and white abolitionists and established her first studio. "I had always wanted to make the forms of things, and while I was at school I tried to make drawings of people and things." She recalled that her mother had invented artistic patterns for embroidery and "perhaps the same thing is coming out in me in a more civilized form."

In 1864, while attending an antislavery meeting, Edmonia Lewis was interviewed by the noted children's writer, Lydia Maria Child. Mrs. Child quoted Lewis on her Indian background:

> No, I have not a single drop of what is called white blood in my veins. My father was a full-blooded Negro, and my mother was a full-blooded Chippewa. . . .
>
> And have you lived with the Chippewas?
>
> Yes. When my mother was dying, she wanted me to promise that I would live three years with her people, and I did.
>
> And what did you do while you were there?
>
> I did as my mother's people did. I made baskets and embroidered moccasins and I went

into the cities with my mother's people to sell them. . . .

Lewis then showed Mrs. Child a bust of Voltaire she was completing, and offered this comment: "I don't want you to go to praise me," she said, "for I know praise is not good for me. Some praise me because I am a colored girl, and I don't want that kind of praise. I had rather you would point out my defects, for that will teach me something."

During her long artistic career in the United States and Europe, Edmonia Lewis asked for and benefited from criticism. Shortly after this interview she left for Europe and established a studio in Rome. She turned out portrait busts of her heroes: Abraham Lincoln; abolitionists Charles Sumner, William L. Garrison, and Maria Chapman; and her favorite white figure, John Brown.

In 1876 her *Death of Cleopatra* was first exhibited at the Philadelphia Centennial Exposition and drew critical praise as "the grandest statue in the exposition." It weighed over two tons, stood twelve feet tall, and took over four years to make. By this time the works of Edmonia Lewis were exhibited and sold from New York and Boston to Minnesota and California, and in Europe.

Her works were commissioned by wealthy patrons, and she became a celebrity whose Rome studio drew tourists and the curious. She was considered an eccentric by some who commented about her "masculine look," careless dress style, and "personal peculiarities."

Edmonia Lewis was a short woman with straight black, abundant hair and "a proud spirit," which she believed came from her mother. She was known for her honest talk about her early hard times.

Visitors to her Rome studio remembered she had a tendency to lapse into "quietude and stoicism." Others recalled a demeanor that showed the "sadness of African and Indian races."

The date and place of her death are not known.

TEXAS AND CALIFORNIA BEFORE THE CIVIL WAR

PLAINS INDIAN NATIONS—THE Comanches, Kiowas, Lipans, and Apaches—became tough, hard-riding people who challenged the European invader on countless battlefields.

They had no slaves and saw foreigners of any color or language as a danger. For them Africans brought West by white masters were part of an enemy advance on their civilization. Both white and black dressed like Europeans, used the same tools, and lived in houses. Slave and master were part of the same tide that would swallow up Native American life on the Great Plains and the deserts of the southwest.

Many slaves, picked for their loyalty before being brought to the wilderness, stood by their masters on the frontier. But despite a master's careful selection, some slaves bolted for freedom at the earliest opportunity.

During Texas's Lone Star Rebellion, Colonel James Morgan reported black slaves were seeking contacts with Texas Indians, and "wished to join the Mexicans," so they could be free. The next year a Mexican General led Biloxi Indians, Mexicans, and African Americans against US whites. In one battle two black men died and one, a large man who spoke French, was captured. He defiantly shouted he had always been free and had no respect for the Texas government. A firing squad promptly shot him.

Luckier was an African American man married to a Native American and living in her village near Carson City, Nevada, in 1860. He was caught running guns, ammunition, and bowie knives to nearby Indians. He admitted to his captors he had been doing it for years and that he had a Quaker partner. Before he was punished, he managed to escape. His Quaker partner was not found.

In California, Africans constituted a significant part of the population under Spanish rule and mixed easily with Native Americans. A Spanish census of 1790 found 18 percent of the population of San Francisco, 24 percent of San Jose, 20 percent of Santa Barbara, and 18 percent of Monterey had African ancestors.

The city of Los Angeles was founded in 1781 by forty-four people, of whom only two were Europeans, and the rest African, Indian, or a mixture of the three races. Maria Rita Valdez, a granddaughter of one black founder, owned a section of land called Beverly Hills. Francisco Reyes, another founder, owned the San Fernando Valley. In the 1790s he sold it and became mayor of Los Angeles.

Black Indians of San Francisco in the 1840s

The governor of California before the arrival of the US armed forces was Pio Pico. Governor Pico came from a prominent California family with African ancestors.

The arrival of US rule changed life in California. Under Spain and Mexico about 15 percent of Californians had listed themselves as African in heritage. This population disappeared on US Census rolls. Slavery, racial animosity, and California's new "Black Laws" drove them to the safe side of the color line.

Little is known about the Black Indians who strode or rode across California's trails after that. One white pioneer remembered a black man preaching to Native Americans in their own language near the Canadian River. He also reported that on the Santa Fe trail black people "have a great deal of influence with the Indians." At Fort Kearny he found a black interpreter using his knowledge of Spanish and Indian languages to provide US authorities with valuable information.

SLAVERY IN THE FIVE NATIONS

THE CHOCTAW, CHICKASAW, CHEROKEE, Creek, and Seminole Nations were early targeted by European merchants, missionaries, and government officials. Because they readily accepted Christianity, and European styles in houses and dress, whites began to call them "The Five Civilized Tribes." With the exception of the Seminoles, some members also became slaveowners.

By 1860 slavery had become a major part of life for the Four Nations, and only the Seminoles firmly rejected bondage in favor of a system of friendship and alliance with their black members. But among the other Four Nations slavery began to shape their development and village life.

Each nation splintered into a wealthy slaveholding minority and a poorer majority. For example, among Cherokees only 12 percent owned slaves. But slaves made up 18 percent of the Cherokees, 14 percent of the Choctaws, 18 percent of the Chickasaws, and 10 percent of the Creeks.

Slavery pushed Native Americans into crucial economic and cultural changes. Before skill and character had counted, but now race became important in judging people. The Cherokees and others adopted "Slave Codes" to control their black men and women, prevent their escape and even their learning to read and write. If a slave ran off or rebelled, Indian Slave Codes required other members of the nation to help catch him or her.

Slavery also altered the basic economies of these nations. Each turned from hunting and fishing to tilling huge plantations with slave labor. This labor surplus produced enough crops to sell in the open market. Slavery had driven four major and benign Indian Nations into capitalist expansion and labor exploitation.

Bondage is always a violation of the human spirit and the will to be free. But most observers found that the chains of slavery fitted rather loosely on African Americans owned by Indians. Only the Chickasaws had a reputation for treating slaves as badly as white masters. The other nations practiced such a mild form of bondage that it upset US slave owners. The Seminoles, of course, infuriated white and Indian masters with their level of generosity, fairness, and equality toward "slaves."

What was bondage like for those held by Native Americans? In interviews conducted during the 1930s, former slaves evaluated their experiences differently. Johnson Thompson, eighty, and a former Cherokee slave, said: "The master never punish anybody, and I never see anybody whipped, and only one slave sold. Lots of slave children didn't ever learn to read."

Rochelle Ward, ninety-one, remembered: "Some of the slaves work around and get money and pay this money to their master for freedom, so there was some freed before the close of the war. Some of the others tried to run away after the war started."

Chaney Rickardson, ninety, recalled: "None of the Cherokees ever whipped us, and my mistress gave me some mighty fine rules to live by. Didn't have no jails for Negroes and no jail for themselves. We all had plenty to eat."

Whites who visited slaveholding Indians described enslaved men and women who were well-treated, adequately fed and cared for. US slaveholders viewed this leniency as a sign Native Americans did not understand bondage. They also thought it posed a danger to their own ability to control their laborers. If Native Americans did not know how to treat slaves, then something would have to be done about Native Americans.

THE TRAIL OF TEARS

FOR WHITE US CITIZENS in the eastern states problems presented by Native Americans were solved in a single dramatic stroke by the Indian Removal Act of 1830. It provided for the mass deportation of the Five Nations from their huge, fertile homelands in the southeast.

Some sixty thousand red and black men and women were

eventually deposited on lands in Arkansas and Oklahoma that whites considered uninhabitable.

Removal meant more than a change of geography. Fragile cultures were uprooted by Army troops and driven to an alien climate and location.

For Cherokees it was a murderous "trail of tears." President Martin Van Buren ordered seven thousand soldiers under General Winfield Scott to move a nation of fourteen thousand. Homes were burned, livestock, tools, printing presses, and personal possessions seized and destroyed.

Cherokee men, women, and children, including one thousand six hundred Black Cherokees were prodded westward in midwinter by Federal bayonets. About ten thousand Cherokees survived, but President Van Buren assured Congress that their expulsion "had the happiest effects. . . . The Cherokees have emigrated without apparent reluctance."

In the Indian Territory the Five Nations, decimated by their deadly journey, faced a wilderness. Clearing was necessary before settlements could survive. Those who had left their dead on the long trail across the South to the Mississippi and beyond now had to turn to building new homes. Only a rich cultural heritage and strong families provided the fortitude necessary to sustain nations.

On their new lands Indians faced new assaults. Whites seeking to profit from their misery appeared in their camps with products to sell. Native Americans became more dependent upon white goods and values. Government "Indian agents" regulated their lives and paved the way for other intruders. Slavery became even more entrenched.

The Indian agents sent by Washington openly encouraged

slaveholding. Soon two distinct classes based on slave owner-ship divided each Indian Nation. "Mixed bloods" owned slaves and usually had some white ancestry. Though a minority, they felt both of these facts made them superior, fit to rule. This also meant the amount of "white" blood was a positive, much as the amount of "black" blood was a negative. "Full bloods" formed a majority, but because they had no white blood and held no slaves, they had little power.

Between 1830 and 1860 the population of the Four Nations declined sharply, Cherokees by 31 percent, Choctaws by 27 percent, Chickasaws by 18 percent, and Creeks by 43 percent. At the same time the number of members with white blood increased and so too did the number of slaves each nation held. By 1860 Cherokees held 2,511, Choctaws 2,344, Creeks 1,532, and Chickasaws 975.

Slavery had become the major economic and political fac-tor in these nations. This meant that their racial thinking was approaching that of the white South.

However, visitors to the Indian Territory reported a type of bondage that hardly matched the harshness and cruelty of the white South.

In 1853 German artist Möllhausen wrote:

> These slaves receive from the Indian masters more Christian treatment than among the Chris-tian whites. The traveler may seek in vain for any other difference between master and servant than such as nature has made in the physical charac-teristics of the races; and the Negro is regarded as a companion and helper, to whom thanks and

kindness are due when he exerts himself for the welfare of the household.

The mild bondage practiced by Indians soon came under sharp attack by neighboring white slaveholders and US Indian agents. Choctaw Agent Douglas Cooper thought that Choctaws, Cherokees, and Creeks should have white US owners of slaves live in their villages and "control matters." (The Chickasaws, it will be remembered, were considered almost as harsh as white masters.)

Elias Rector, Superintendent of Southern Indian Affairs in 1859, had another thought. He suggested that every Indian family should own slaves because it would tend "to civilize them." He also believed Indians would benefit from black slaves "who could teach them to cultivate the soil and properly prepare and cook their foods."

Though whites became upset at the leniency of Indian slavery, some slaves themselves reached a different conclusion. At four in the morning, on November 15, 1842, African American men and women on Cherokee land owned by the Vann family near Weber Falls mutinied. Creek and Cherokee slaves locked overseers

Sac Fox women

in cabins, seized guns, horses, and provisions and then gathered up their children for a dash to Mexico. Black Seminoles were suspected of having sparked the rebellion.

An estimated 60 to 250 slaves joined a liberation march singing "I'll tell you, Marsa Ben, your Niggers gwine to leave you!" Armed Cherokees mounted up and rode after them, but were defeated in a two-day battle. Finally, fresh Cherokee troops arrived to overwhelm the rebels on an open prairie. The survivors were brought back, some to be executed, others whipped.

That same year hunters on the Washita River reported a fort garrisoned by one to two hundred runaway slaves from the Indian Territory. For the next eighteen years whites believed "outlaw negroes" were responsible for murders along the Choctaw border.

To the extent that some Native Americans adopted a mean-spirited, profit-hungry slavery urged on them by whites and Indian agents, they faced the same rebelliousness that marked the southern states. But, despite the inducements and pressures, most rejected that foreign standard and followed their own gentler instincts. This simple decision stands as yet another example of a treasured independent spirit by Native Americans. The beneficiaries were the African Americans whose slave years were spent with people who found it very difficult to treat other human beings as pieces of property.

THE FINEST SPECIMENS OF MANKIND

THE CIVIL WAR PITTED brother against brother, and nowhere more painfully than among the Five Nations. "Mixed bloods," committed to slavery clashed with "full bloods" and their black allies who just wanted to be left in peace.

The Indian Territory in 1861 was surrounded by the Confederacy and flooded with its agents and sympathizers. Most federal agents in the Indian Territory favored slavery and the Confederacy. Then Confederate officials and troops arrived to control matters and US power was nowhere in sight. By the time Fort Sumter surrendered that April, Chickasaws and Choctaws had signed treaties with the Confederacy. Cherokees, Creeks, and Seminoles were told by Confederate officials "there ain't no more US—ain't any more Treaty—all be dead." By August leaders of these nation's leaders had caved in and allied their members to the new Confederacy.

≫| |≪

THESE NATIVE AMERICANS FAVORING neutrality or the Union (including most black members) grouped around a wealthy Creek Chief, Opothle Yahola. He secretly wrote to President Lincoln asking for the protection promised, saying "now the wolf has come. Men who are strangers tread our soil. Our children are frightened & mothers cannot sleep for fear." Getting this letter to the Union forces proved almost impossible. Getting Union help in 1861 was impossible.

Opothle Yahola and his followers hoped to live out the war in peace. They moved away from pro-Confederate Indians and camped out on the Indian Territory's southwestern frontier—men, women, and children with stores of food, livestock, wagons, and possessions. Half of the Seminole Nation joined them, as well as blacks from all Five Nations and Kickapoos, Shawnees, Delawares, and Comanches.

Confederate Creek soldiers wanted to attack the camp and seize Opothle Yahola as a traitor. Douglas Cooper, US Indian agent, now serving as commander of Indian Confederate troops, restrained them.

Finally when Cooper's forces advanced on the camp with troops composed of Choctaws, Creeks, Chickasaws, and white Texas cavalry regiments, it was deserted. The "peace" Indians had picked up and left on a long trail. The Confederate forces assumed they were headed toward Union lines in Kansas. Actually they were circling around searching for other pro-peace or pro-Union Cherokees.

The week before Thanksgiving, Confederates tracked down the Opothle Yahola party near Stillwater and attacked. The peace forces regrouped and continued their march into the Cherokee Nation. Two weeks later Cooper's regiments, including fresh Cherokee troops, caught up with them. When the battle began these Cherokee soldiers deserted to the peace band.

This larger conglomeration of neutral Indians made their headquarters and built a stronghold north of Tulsa. The day after Christmas Confederate troops again attacked and desperate hand-to-hand fighting began.

The peace forces were defeated and fled, abandoning wagons, bedding, and clothing. They lost about 900 cattle, 250 ponies, and 190 sheep and took off on foot through a blizzard toward Kansas and the Union lines. Desperate men tried to cover the retreat of their women and children with weapons they found. Said one Seminole chief "At that battle we lost everything we possessed, everything to take care of our women and children with, and all that we had. . . . We left them in cold blood by the wayside."

During the fighting and forced march many froze to death. Bodies were devoured by wolves.

After a long forced march, the survivors reached Kansas and had to camp without blankets on ground that was still frozen. Once he had been a rich man, owning many slaves and cattle, but now Apothle Yahola had lost his daughter on the daring march, and he was very ill. He died within a year, knowing he had led a bold exodus for freedom through the winter snows. By April, as the first buds of spring came through the soil, some 7,600 in his camp were receiving US Army supplies and his men were talking of enlisting as Union soldiers.

One of the first regiments formed by the surviving men was led by Jim Lane, a flamboyant Kansas senator. Only five years

Senator Jim Lane of Kansas recruited men to fight for the Union from among the red and black Seminoles and Creeks who fought their way from the Indian Territory.

earlier Lane publicly stated that the African was a connecting link between human and orangutan. After leading his Black Indians into battle he changed his tune. He now believed they were "the finest specimens of manhood I have ever gazed upon."

FREEDOM COMES TO THE FIVE NATIONS

THE DEFEAT OF THE Confederacy gave the US government a new opportunity to impose its will on Native Americans, since most had become allies of the Confederacy. Existing treaties were scrapped. A large portion of Indian Territory was taken from the Five Nations by the Federal government and handed to the Plains Nations, Shawnees, and Delawares.

Emancipation also was imposed from outside. The US government and white citizens had once demanded Native Americans adopt slavery and hunt runaways. Now they demanded that all slaves of Indians become free and equal. The white man had again spoken with forked tongue.

Seminoles, whose African Americans often had been dear friends and family members, quickly accepted emancipation and equality. Soon Cherokees and Creeks did. Choctaws resisted for a generation and Chickasaws fought the issue almost to the end of the century. Except for the Seminoles, within each nation black members faced years of legal challenges and political protests to win citizenship rights, land, education, and equality of opportunity. The African American effort in the Indian Territory reflected their wider and less successful campaign for equality during this era of Reconstruction in the southern states.

Among the Seminoles, African Americans were immediately liberated and six were elected to the forty-two-seat Seminole Council. By the end of freedom's first year Black Seminoles were building homes, churches, schools, and businesses, planting and harvesting crops. Parents showed an avid interest in education for their children, and some adults attended night schools.

Black members of other Indian Nations worked vigorously for equality, land ownership, and education. Very few left their host nation. Whatever unfairness they felt among their Indian friends could not match what they knew they would experience among whites. They knew this and stayed. Here were people who would never lynch or brutalize their sons and daughters.

Among Creeks, Seminoles, and Cherokees, African

Americans made economic strides they could rarely duplicate in US society. Black Cherokees owned barbershops, blacksmith shops, general stores, and restaurants. Some had become printers, ferry-boat operators, cotton-gin managers, teachers, and postmasters.

As early as 1866, John B. Sanborn, Commissioner of Indian Affairs, reported from the Indian Territory:

> The freedmen are the most industrious, economical, and in many respects, the more intelligent portion of the population of the Indian Territory. They all desire to remain in that territory upon lands set apart for their own exclusive use.

Even as ex-slaves among Cherokees, Creeks, and Seminoles were making these rapid strides, those among the Choctaws and Chickasaws suffered. Black men who had fought for the Union during the Civil War found they and their families were denied full membership. Commissioner Sanborn found it was "not safe or advisable" for some former soldiers to even return to their villages. Conditions in these nations changed very slowly.

The black thirst for education that blossomed throughout the former slave states bloomed among the Five Nations as well. Collecting money from poor but interested parents, Black Indians built their own schools, hired and paid teachers, and then asked for additional government aid. An 1866 government report on Black Creeks revealed they "are anxious that their children shall be educated" and are "determined to profit" from "the school formed at their own advance."

The first choice of Black Indians was to have their children

Early Oklahoma school for children of color

educated in the same classrooms as other members of their nation. But that plan often failed, and so they sought funds to begin their own schools. When even that failed, and often before, they converted homes and churches into schools.

They were urged on by educated professionals among their members. O. S. Fox, editor of the Cherokee *Afro-American Advocate* wrote: "If you have to make a sacrifice make it and fill that school up. To be anything the Indian must be educated."

Arthur Bean wrote in his agreement: "By all means let us have some sort of school. I say that he is no man at all who cannot pay one dollar a month to have his children educated."

Slowly but surely, the Five Nations, even the resistant

Chickasaws, agreed to provide financial support for Black Indian schools. By 1907 Chickasaws operated twenty-one schools for black members, and some were integrated.

The Black Indian campaign for full citizenship was carried on with forceful but respectful language. In 1879 a group of Black Cherokees petitioned for equal rights:

> The Cherokee nation is our country; there we were born and reared; there are our homes made by the sweat of our brows; there are our wives and children, whom we love as dearly as though we were born with red, instead of black skins. There we intend to live and defend our natural rights, as guaranteed by the treaties and laws of the United States, by every legitimate and lawful means.

Even as they pressured and demanded, O. S. Fox reminded his fellow Black Indians of the benefits of remaining among their nation's friends:

> The opportunities for our people in that country far surpassed any of the kind possessed by our people in the US . . . It is nonsense for any Afro-American to emigrate to Africa or any-where else if he can make a living in the Indian Territory.

In 1884, as the Chickasaw Nation argued the merits of granting equality to black members, a convention of Black

Chickasaws met and affirmed their loyalty to the nation:

> As natives, we are attached to the people among whom we have been born and bred. We like the Chickasaws as friends and we know by the experience of the past that we can live with them in the future in a close union. . . .

At the end of the Civil War and for a variety of reasons, many African Americans left white society to enter Indian Nations. Thousands stayed to marry Indian women or men, raise children, and make their living in an accepting culture that was not burdened with hatreds based on skin color. Since so many remained, it can be assumed that they found a greater fulfillment there than elsewhere.

During this time many white people also joined Indian Nations. Some people of both races were probably attracted by the cash or land offerings the US government made to settle accounts with Native Americans. But beyond these self-seekers were many who concluded that Native Americans understood freedom, family, and law better than the surrounding societies of the day.

FROM TERRITORY TO STATEHOOD

US CITIZENS FIRST BECAME aware of good grasslands in the Indian Territory during the great cattle drives that passed through to Kansas after the Civil War. By 1872, the railroad had sent its iron horse chugging through Oklahoma's fertile plains. Now there was no stopping land-hungry pioneers. By the

1880s the US government and its mounted infantry and cavalry regiments formed a thin blue line of protection against white intruders.

But there was no stemming this lust for settlement. A dream of land and an appetite for economic gain had always powered the white pioneer spirit. It soon collided with a Federal pledge to keep Native Americans safe on these lands. A white "boomer" invasion began in 1880, truculently crashing through to build camps, only to be ejected by the US Army. White and black soldiers, often reluctantly, escorted boomers out each time.

The boomers grew to an estimated forty thousand, and most swore an oath to keep fighting until Oklahoma was theirs. By 1889, the government joined the movement and forced both Creeks and Seminoles to surrender their land rights in return for cash. An Oklahoma land rush was organized for US citizens.

On April 22, 1889, an estimated one hundred thousand men, women, and children on horses, bicycles, buggies, in wheelbarrows and on foot lined up for the shot that would lead to their dream of land. About ten thousand were African Americans.

In a few hours a "vacant" land had been settled. In a year Oklahoma became a US, not an Indian, Territory.

One of the most daring black characters to arrive was Edwin P. McCabe, described as a "handsome man of Indian complexion." He had been elected to two terms as Kansas State Auditor only to have his fellow Republicans deny him renomination for a third term. McCabe reached Oklahoma with some concrete plans and a special vision. He wanted to transform it into a black state perhaps with himself as territorial and then state governor.

To that end, McCabe applied his considerable talents in business and politics. He believed that with proper encouragement

Edwin P. McCabe

enough southern black migrants might pour into Oklahoma to form a voting majority in each election district. To help matters along he founded the town of Lang-ston as a headquarters for the effort. It became one of thirty-two black towns that mushroomed in Oklahoma between 1890 and 1910.

In his impeccable three-piece suit McCabe watched the black population rise to 137,000 by 1910. But he also saw his hopes dashed by an old foe.

From the beginning whites made it clear they would not have people of color flexing their political muscles in Oklahoma. In 1890, the *Kansas City News,* under the headline "Oklahoma As a Negro State," reported whites "almost foam at the mouth whenever McCabe's name is suggested for Governor [and] also at the idea of negroes getting control. . . ." The *New York Times* reported from Oklahoma that McCabe might be "assassinated within a week" and quoted a white settler saying, "I would not give five cents for his life."

McCabe realized how futile his hope for the governorship

Boley—founded in 1904 by Abigail Barnett, a Black Choctaw—became one of thirty-two African American towns started in Oklahoma from the time of its land rush in 1889 to 1910. This is the town council of Boley, with its mayor in the center and the sheriff in the far left of the rear.

was and concentrated on building a vigorous black Oklahoma. He organized his people in Langston for another land rush in September 1891. That day McCabe was fired on by three whites and only rescued by black citizens wielding Winchesters.

McCabe was later picked to serve in a minor state office, but left his job the day Oklahoma became a state in the Union. It was hardly the Oklahoma of opportunity he had envisioned.

Black residents tried mightily to prevent Oklahoma from becoming another segregationist southern state. They formed the Equal Rights Association, the Suffrage League, the Afro-American League, the Negro Protective League, and local protest associations. Their sentiments can be seen in the words of the Equal Rights Association of Kingfisher County meeting in convention in 1904:

> We pledge ourselves to resist to the bitter end the efforts of our deadly enemies in attempting to mold a sentiment against us after the southern method.
>
> Our deadly foes are now busy educating their children to hate us and to believe that we are low, degraded, and vicious because our skins are dark.

The march of history in the form of huge white migrations crushed the ambitious hopes of Oklahomans of color. Each section of land opened to settlement led to Native Americans and African Americans becoming more outnumbered, more restricted.

A Federal government that had once promised Indians territorial integrity and security "forever" now forced entire native reservations into individual holdings. Unfamiliar with private property and a legal system based on it, Indians saw their lands slip into white hands. They became dispossessed from their own territory, with white speculators reaping the rewards.

Black Indians called the black newcomers to their region "state negroes." It is unclear if either African American population moved toward making common cause. When three hundred black Oklahomans met in convention at Muskogee in December, 1906 they protested election of an all-white Oklahoma Constitutional Convention. But among the people who wrote this proud statement were there African Americans and Black

Indians united?: "In this territory, white man, red man, and black man have always lived in perfect harmony; no hideous lynchings mar the good name of the Territory; no mob violence to destroy, frighten or drive off outside investors. . . ." When these three hundred delegates pointed out that blacks numbered about "80,000, owning quite a million acres, possessing a personal and real property to the value of two million and upward," were they counting their brothers and sisters who lived among Native Americans? It is unclear.

What is clear is that Oklahoma entered the Union as the forty-sixth state, but not as a haven for all people. Its Black Indians could not vote and its African Americans faced violence if they tried to vote. Dark citizens of the state could not sit with whites in school, public buildings, railroad cars, or elsewhere. Oklahoma became the first state to segregate telephone booths.

President Theodore Roosevelt, noted for his "Square Deal," signed the document admitting Oklahoma to statehood in November 1907. Edwin P. McCabe's vision of Oklahoma crashed to earth with a thud, but the spirited man was not finished.

Three months after statehood, McCabe went to court to challenge Oklahoma's right to segregate railroad passengers by race. He may have reasoned that a solid legal victory against segregation on trains could topple an entire discriminatory system.

Court after court ruled against McCabe, and still he carried his case forward on appeal. He sold his Oklahoma home, possibly to raise money for his legal costs, and left the state. Or perhaps he was in some danger.

Finally, in 1914, the Supreme Court ruled in the case of *E. P. McCabe, et al. v. Atchison, Topeka and Santa Fe Railroad Company, et al.* Segregation, it said, was legal not only on Oklahoma trains but everywhere else.

McCabe's political career, like the rights of black Oklahomans, was over. He moved to Chicago and soon slipped into poverty. He died a pauper in 1920 at age seventy. His wife managed to scrape together enough money to bring McCabe's body back to Topeka, Kansas, scene of his greatest political triumph—where he was twice elected to state office. He was interred in the presence of his wife, a white undertaker, and a gravedigger.

The year before McCabe died, seventy-six black people were lynched and twenty-five cities exploded in antiblack violence. His dream for Oklahoma might have saved some of those who lost their lives or suffered injuries.

In the years before McCabe's death, another man announced a grandiose plan to rescue black people from their enemies in the Americas. Marcus Garvey, a black Jamaican, whose ancestors had fought as maroons, proposed a massive African American exodus to Africa, the ancestral homeland.

Garvey, like McCabe, had concluded African Americans needed an escape hatch. But for the Jamaican there was no safe place in the United States or anywhere in the Western Hemisphere for black people. Even as black settlers had poured into Oklahoma in the 1890s at McCabe's urging, some soon decided the West was no safer than the East. One group packed their belongings and left for New York City and ships that carried them to Africa. They had come to Garvey's conclusion.

NO BARS CAN HOLD CHEROKEE BILL

WHEN THE INDIAN TERRITORY became Oklahoma it lurched from a possible haven for people of color to another white supremacist state. More died than just a dream. The young among Native American of every color suffered the most, for their future had been shut down. In their frustration and pain they slipped off to drink a lot or sleep excessively. To avoid family quarrels that grew more frequent and bitter, some left for the open road. A few turned to a life of crime.

In their own flamboyant, perverted ways our young criminals represent the societies from which they spring. They express their communities blocked goals. This helps explain why citizens see certain crooks as the crude cutting edge of a people's justice system. They ramble along settling scores and shouting for the powerless from the cold steel of a gun barrel or knife blade.

Robin Hood became a medieval hero for Saxon peasants oppressed by heartless nobles and an evil king in England. Frank and Jesse James were rural thieves whose daring holdups were judged a fair response to railroad owners who cheated western farmers. During the Great Depression, many US citizens, infuriated that banks had swallowed their money, glamourized wild and selfish bank robbers.

To be Indian or African here historically has meant a twisted relationship with the law. Europeans, seeking to increase their holdings and wealth at the expense of people of color, set all the economic and legal rules of the game. Land seizures and slavery became perfectly legal, and nonwhite resistance in any form became illegal. Law, the justice system, and military power protected their needs from nonwhite discontent.

From the beginning some dark people abandoned any effort to live by the law, even their own peoples' sense of justice. Called "outlaws," they took up sword and musket and became outlaws. It would be strange indeed if a brutal system produced only gracious victims, men and women who met dishonesty and injustice with a shrug, and humiliation with a smile.

From the earliest maroon resistance in the Americas, oppression and pain created evil monsters as well as intrepid heroes. Many, many times a people's politics would slip into crime. And noble figures have employed excessive violence to further a just cause. Some criminals have paused in their mayhem to defend innocent victims.

In the 1880s Dick Glass led his cattle-rustling, bootlegging desperadoes into a shooting war to protect Black Creeks victimized by Cherokee "half bloods." Then he led them back to their old ways.

In the next decade wild rampages by young Cherokee Bill and an even younger Rufus Buck gang came at a moment of deep political frustration for their kin, Black Cherokees and Creeks.

One senses in their frantic rage a muddled objection to dispossessed people again being told to get out or lie low.

THE DICK GLASS RUSTLER GANG

THE INDIAN TERRITORY AFTER the Civil War was host to many fugitives from justice. Criminals poured in from around the country and residents called their soil "the land of the six-shooter." In 1874 Fort Smith's *Western Independent* published this eyewitness account of life:

> We have lived in and around the Indian country since the Spring of 1834, but have never known such a state of terror. Now it is murder throughout the length and breadth of the Indian country. It has been the rendezvous of the vile and wicked from everywhere, an inviting field for murder and robbery, because it is the highway between Texas, Missouri, Kansas and Arkansas.

By the time a tall, gloomy Judge Isaac Parker arrived to build his reputation as a "hanging judge," there had been fifty or more murders without arrests within fourteen months. "There's no God west of Fort Smith," said local citizens.

One lively source of trouble since the Civilized Nations first adopted slavery was the struggle between bigoted "mixed bloods" and Black Indians. By 1878 Cherokee mixed bloods were in a shooting war against Black Creeks across their invisible border. Cherokee gunmen targeted Creek Lighthorsemen, their local police.

Cherokees galloped into Creek lands to defy police authority and fire into Creek homes. By early 1880 Creeks claimed Cherokee desperadoes had slain four and wounded six people for racial reasons. When they demanded legal action, nothing happened.

For some reason, Dick Glass, whose outlaw band ruled nearby Marshalltown, decided to help out. When two Black Creeks, implicated in stealing horses, were kidnapped and lynched on Cherokee soil, Glass leaped to action. Perhaps the two were friends or members of his gang.

On the morning of July 27, 1880, Glass led his outlaws across the border into Cherokee territory and a gunfight began. Several men on both sides were wounded and Glass was shot through the cheekbone and lost his horse to Cherokee fire.

Feelings escalated on both sides. A Cherokee court found the suspects in the Creek lynchings innocent. Rewards were posted for Dick Glass, wanted dead or alive, and he had to abandon Marshalltown and the Cherokee region.

He took up trading stolen horses in Denison, Texas, for liquor which he sold in the dry Indian Territory at high prices. There was a $300 fine for selling liquor to Native Americans, but it flowed freely anyway.

In 1882 Glass had a wild shoot-out with Creek Lighthorsemen that left him so badly wounded, he was reported dead. Later that year he was captured by a Kansas sheriff seeking the $600 reward. But Glass mysteriously escaped, probably by bribing the lawman.

At the year's end Glass was again on the trail in defense of his people, leading a column of Black Creeks in the Green Peach War against mixed bloods. Then, after two years of no news about him, Glass sent a long, curious letter to the Commissioner of Indian Affairs. He denied any criminal activity and claimed he was blamed for the evil deeds of others.

His statement was well organized, clear, and his only effort to exonerate himself from the serious charges against him:

> I have been hounded for nearly five years with a reward on me dead or alive. I have been obliged to hide . . . [and others have committed crimes] and lay it on me, knowing I dare not come forward and prove my innocense for fear someone might assassinate me, as has been done to two of my companions. . . .

Glass then said his troubles stemmed from a grudge people had against him because he was black. "Had I been an Indian," he wrote, no charges would have been placed against his good name.

No one believed Dick Glass then, and it is difficult to believe him now. He was in the business of rustling cattle and selling illegal liquor. Although he apparently tried to avoid killing people, he was little more than a desperado. Historian Kenneth W. Porter has suggested, "If Robin Hood, legendary outlaw-champion of the Saxon peasantry, ever existed as a historical character, he probably resembled Dick Glass more than he did the Robin Hoods of ballads, novels and movies."

Dick Glass died as he lived, in a hail of bullets. Carrying a wagon of whiskey into the Chickasaw Nation in 1885, his gang ran into Sam Sixkiller and two other US deputy marshals. In the inevitable shoot-out Glass died of bullet wounds.

Glass, like the rest of us, would prefer to be remembered for good deeds rather than bad. But his defense of his race was a short-lived, part-time job during a long life of crime.

CHEROKEE BILL

SAGAS OF THE OLD West reserve a special place for the best shot, worst outlaw, and most feared gunman. Billy the Kid usually is handed one of these awards, if not all. The only photograph of this mass murderer who killed twenty-one men before he died at twenty, shows a sloppy, bucktoothed, moronic young thug. But after his death, this psychopathic thrill-killer received a new life as a heroic fantasy. When Hollywood glorified his career in horse operas, it picked handsome actors such as Robert Taylor, Emilio Estevez, and Paul Newman to play Billy the Kid as a good guy.

What the real Billy the Kid lacked in looks, height, and bearing, a tall, charming, and handsome Cherokee Bill had in real life. But he proved quite as lethally dangerous as his white counterpart.

Cherokee Bill was born Crawford Goldsby in 1876 to George Goldsby, sergeant in the famed US Tenth Cavalry Regiment, and Ellen Beck, both Black Cherokees. With his parents at Fort Concho, Texas, he entered a world of frontier law and order.

Two years after Bill was born, turmoil struck the Goldsby home when his father was accused of permitting his black soldiers to take carbines to settle a dispute with some white Texans. To avoid trial his father disappeared. (White Texans often taunted and even shot at the African American soldiers who guarded their towns and homesteads. And furious bluecoats returned the fire when they could.)

As young Bill grew older, this incident could have nagged him with sharp questions about a justice system that drives a father from his wife and baby boy. Mrs. Goldsby, seeking work, moved Bill and his younger brother from one place to another. The two boys were often left without parental guidance.

But his mother did enroll Bill for three years in a Cherokee, Kansas, school and for two more years at the Carlisle Indian school in far-off Pennsylvania. When Cherokee Bill returned home at twelve, his mother was living in the Indian Territory and had remarried a man with whom Bill could not get along.

Left alone much of the time, the only recorded advice Bill received from his mother was, "Stand up for your rights. Don't let anybody impose on you." That would not be his problem.

The young man began to explore the rough frontier life and his Cherokee heritage. He grew into a burly, six-foot teenager, quick to smile and make friends, and devastatingly attractive to women. In 1894 he was eighteen and so far had managed to stay out of trouble on a lawless frontier.

But if he was sensitive to the plight of his Cherokee people, he saw their trouble was mounting. Aggressive white settlers gobbled up Indian lands as fast as the US government seized or bought them. In 1893 Cherokees were pushed into the process of losing their best lands and settling for payments of $265.70 each.

These payments began on June 4,1894, and by this time, Cherokee Bill was on a rampage that made him number one on the US marshal's "wanted list." Rewards for him totaled a staggering $1,300.

Cherokee Bill's life of crime began at a dance with a fistfight with black Jake Lewis. Thrashed in a fair fight, Bill came roaring back two days later, guns blazing and put two bullets in Lewis. He then fled to the hill country and joined the Jim and Bill Cook outlaw band. When a posse attacked their hideout, Cherokee Bill picked off one posseman. He had his first notch.

From that point on Cherokee Bill acted as though he knew he was destined to die in two years and wanted to kill as many men as he could. He murdered a barber during a bank holdup and then formed his own band. Then he wiped out a station agent in Nowata, a conductor on a train near Fort Gibson, and an unarmed onlooker during a post office holdup at Lenapah. Because the man was a prominent citizen, this last senseless slaying proved to be his undoing.

Cherokee Bill was often protected from harm by loyal friends and a violent reputation. Lawmen who pursued him, hearing of his fast six-shooter action, kept a safe distance and avoided engaging him in battle. Because he was on good terms with Cherokees, Creeks, and Seminoles, he moved easily through their villages and lands, something his pursuers often could not do. And he always found women who offered warmth and shelter at night.

In time Cherokee Bill's crimes became so infamous and documented that investigators stopped collecting evidence. The problem was catching him.

Cherokee Bill and the Bill Cook gang paused in their criminal careers to try to collect their $265.70 government share for confiscated Cherokee lands. They realized their appearance in Tahlequah to collect the money would lead to a shoot-out. Instead they wrote out their money orders and sent them along with Effie Crittendon, a friend. She was handed the money but then followed back to the Cook hideout by lawmen seeking the desperadoes.

A gunfight began and when the smoke had cleared, Jim Cook had been wounded and captured. But Bill Cook and Cherokee Bill had escaped.

With long black hair falling to his shoulders and a smile on his face, the witty, handsome young man cheerfully rode off to further crimes. When not busy robbing people, he was known for his storytelling abilities, singing of ditties, and dancing of jigs. A white rancher who spent a day with him found Cherokee Bill "as full of life and the joy of living as ever passed this way."

Women not only found him alluring, but provided him with places to hide. But a Black Cherokee girlfriend, Maggie Glass, was the cause of his capture. She invited him over one night along with her kin, Ike Rogers, who was a US deputy marshal. When Rogers tried to surprise him, the two men scuffled, Maggie watched, and Bill was finally felled with a chunk of wood.

On the way to jail, Bill broke his handcuffs and leaped from Rogers's wagon. A calm rifle convinced him to climb slowly back.

Brought before Judge Isaac Parker's court at Fort Smith under heavy guard, Cherokee Bill was still unrepentant. His presence soon attracted a large, curious crowd. "No bars can hold Cherokee," pal Bill Cook boasted.

Judge Parker heard his case, sentenced him to death for the murder of the bystander at Lenapah, and sent him down to the dank cell beneath the courthouse. His lawyer immediately filed an appeal to the Supreme Court for a new trial. The outlaw's own appeal, perhaps to his mother, got a smuggled six-gun into

Black Indian and white deputy sheriffs finally managed to bring Cherokee Bill to justice.

his cell. He broke out, and shooting wildly, killed one deputy and wounded others before being recaptured.

This time Judge Parker looked at the face before him and told him that in twenty-one years on the bench at Fort Smith, and after sending dozens upon dozens to the gallows, Cherokee Bill was different: "You are undoubtedly the most ferocious monster, and your record more atrocious than all the criminals who have hitherto stood before this bar."

The judge was not finished. He fulminated, using such phrases as "your ferocity," "bloodshed," "bloodthirsty band," "your passion for crime," and interest in "burn, pillage and destroy." Expressing his regret that he had no worse remedy than execution, he again sentenced the desperado to die, on March 17, 1896. Bill's second appeal to the Supreme Court, like the first, was rejected.

This time there was no smuggled gun, no jailbreak. No more people would die fighting Cherokee Bill or merely standing in his way. According to a local newspaper the condemned man awakened "at 6, singing and whistling." His mother accompanied her son to a gallows in a courtyard packed with one hundred witnesses.

Cherokee Bill, cool to the last, looked at the crowd and joked "looks like something is going to happen." Between ages eighteen and twenty he had killed a dozen men and left others wounded and bleeding. Asked if he had any last words to offer to the assembled crowd, he answered calmly "No, I came here to die—not to make a speech."

THE RUFUS BUCK GANG

THE RUFUS BUCK GANG, a mixture of black and red Creek Indians, killed, killed, and killed again. They apparently never claimed their deadly spree involved a racial, political, or other higher motive. There was no reason or plan behind their pathological outburst. One man claims a member announced they wanted to drive whites from Oklahoma, but offers no evidence for this.

Rufus Buck, Sam Sampson, Maoma July, Lewis and Luckey Davis all had records of minor juvenile crimes and each had been sent to jail by Judge Parker. But that was kid's stuff.

Their murder rampage of thirteen days that began on July 28, 1895, set a record. They killed more people than the famous Starr and Dalton gangs combined, and terrorized everyone in their path.

They began by murdering a Black Indian US deputy marshal, John Garrett, near Okmulgee. It was said he had been keeping his detective's eye on them.

Then they started their awesome work in earnest, killing ranchers, small storekeepers, widows, farmers, and even a child. They took cash, gold watches, clothing, and boots, but theft was just an afterthought. They were enjoying themselves.

They once voted three to two to let a white child live. Another time they shot a black child in the back. At the Hassan farm Rufus Buck announced "I'm Cherokee Bill's brother." Then they forced Mrs. Hassan to prepare a huge meal, ate it, and then raped her, holding her husband at bay with Winchesters. This crime and the murder of lawman Garrett would carry them to the gallows.

On a warm August day a huge posse of Black Creek police, Indians, and whites finally trapped the five young men in a cave, and after a savage gun battle, they surrendered. None of the five had suffered a wound.

Huge crowds gathered to witness their two-day trial. Five defense attorneys were assigned to defend the youths, and one admitted to the jury, "You have heard the evidence. I have nothing to say." Judge Isaac Parker sentenced the desperadoes to die on July 1, 1896. Their case was appealed to the Supreme Court but a new trial was denied.

The day before their execution a photographer captured their mood. Slouching casually, smirking a bit, none showed any remorse for their hideous crime wave. None exhibited any fear of the fate that awaited them the next day. Except for the handcuffs holding them together, they might be mistaken for a junior high school athletic team. There is no demented look, no savage ferocity on their faces, just a few young men hanging out.

On the gallows the next day the young men were quiet, except

The Rufus Buck gang and its leader, Luckey Davis (second from right) rolled up a record worse than the infamous Dalton and Starr gangs. This photograph is of their next to last day on earth.

for Luckey Davis who, spotting his sister in the crowd, shouted, "Good-bye, Martha." Then with the sudden release of trapdoors, less than a year after their thirteen-day shooting spree began, it was all over.

Citizens of every color agreed that Oklahoma and the Indian Territory were a little safer after the traps were sprung.

Midway between the hangings of Cherokee Bill on March 17 and the Rufus Buck gang on July 1, the same Supreme Court that had denied their appeals, spoke on a weightier matter. On

May 17 it issued a landmark Constitutional decision on discrimination against minorities in the United States. In *Plessey v. Ferguson* it ruled seven to one that segregation anywhere in the country was not illegal or unconstitutional. "Separate but equal" became the law of the land, and a legal trick that lasted until the high court overturned it in 1954 in the *Brown v. Board of Education* decision.

This killed any last hope that emancipation might mean equal opportunity and justice for dark people. After a bloody Civil War, decades of talk, legislation, and three Constitutional Amendments promising equality and justice, a legal lid was clamped tightly over the aspirations of people of color.

Perhaps there is no connection between the Supreme Court's decision and the violent careers of Cherokee Bill and the Rufus Buck gang—just a coincidence of time. But maybe young Black Indians might have seen it coming in the government seizure and sale of their lands to white pioneers and the hate heaped on them by mixed bloods.

Perhaps their blindly senseless criminal rampages are partly an impotent, violent scream against this last denial of hope. The appearance at the same moment in history of the most violent Black Indian outbreaks in the United States and the high court's decision may not be totally accidental.

OFFICERS OF THE LAW

FOR EVERY BLACK INDIAN or African American man he sent to the gallows, Judge Isaac Parker sent two or more to the Indian Territory as US deputy marshals. Countless others served the Indian Nations as Lighthorsemen or local mounted police.

One of Judge Parker's earliest actions on arriving at Fort Smith in 1875 was to hire two hundred deputy marshals. Neither race nor color guided his strong hand. As a young congressmen, Parker was known as the "Indian's Best Friend." In twenty-one years as the law west of Fort Smith, his war against crime was colorblind.

The Indian Territory's seventy-four thousand square miles needed a steady judicial hand. Desperate communities offered outlaws asylum in exchange for "immunity" from attacks. Towns feared to have marshals spend the night lest some desperado take offense. Resisting arrest, since it only cost a felon one more year in jail, was common.

From this turbulent land Judge Parker selected a host of dark-skinned deputy marshals: John Garrett, Bill Colbert, Robert Love, John Joss, Eugene Walker, Dick Roebuck, Ike Rogers, Morgan Tucker, Grant Johnson, Bob Fortune, Neely Factor, and Bass Reeves. Lawmen started at $500 or less a year, but could earn extra money on bounties. They could also end up dead.

Black Indian deputy marshals of the Indian Territory

Bass Reeves

Judge Parker and his deputies tried to enforce the law with an even hand. But Federal officials, from the Supreme Court and the president down, sought an Indian Territory safe for white pioneers and business people. The lives and concerns of people of color hardly mattered. Speaking about Native Americans at this time, T. J. Morgan, a Commissioner of Indian Affairs, put the issue bluntly: "We ask them to recognize that we are the better race; that our God is the true God; that our civilization is the better; that our manners and customs are superior."

The best known of Judge Parker's black deputy marshals, Bass Reeves, served the court from his arrival at Fort Smith until Oklahoma entered the Union in 1907. Reeves rode off for thirty-seven years to enforce the law, and only one man, Hellubee Smith, ever slipped through the nets he cast.

Reeves claimed he used clever disguises and detective skills and avoided shoot-outs. However, he admitted killing fourteen men, those that drew on him first. He survived lawless frontier years. A button was shot off his shirt, a belt was shot in two, his hat brim was shot off, and his horse's bridle reins were sliced by bullets.

But Reeves was never wounded. For a lawman sitting on his favorite sorrel horse in a dangerous land, that was more than miraculous. It was downright lucky. Reeves also had a reputation for speaking Native American languages and studying their ways of life.

A six-gun, a disguise or two, a fast steed, and a perceptive understanding of the communities he served, made Bass Reeves's career a successful one. His story is an Oklahoma legend.

"WE ARE IDENTICAL"

DRIVEN TOGETHER BY THE invader, Native Americans and Africans began to find that they shared common birthrights and lives based on family, community, and spirituality. As they embraced, they tried to understand both the grasping nature of the foreign foe and how to survive his onslaught.

TALES OF AID AND COMFORT

JOSIAH HENSON, THE REAL Uncle Tom of Harriet Beecher Stowe's famous 1852 novel, escaped bondage in Kentucky with the aid of Native Americans. His 1849 narrative of his life reveals how local Indians gave him food and a wigwam and helped him make his way northward to Canada.

In 1852, Martin R. Delany, the father of black nationalism in the United States, paused in a denunciation of slavery to say of Indians: "We are identical as the subject of American wrongs, outrages, and oppression, and therefore one in interest." In his novel *Blake or the Huts of America*, Delany's protagonist, Henry, asks Culver, an elderly Native American leader in Texas, "in case that blacks should rise" in rebellion, should they "have hope or fear from the Indian?" Culver reminds him of the fighting Seminole alliance in Florida and of the intermarriage "that winds around and holds us together," and foresees a future "stout and strong . . . that you can't separate." He concludes, "You must fight" the white foe.

After the Civil War, members of each race found ways to help one another. African American frontier women often took the lead. After Clara Brown gained her freedom, she reached Denver by covered wagon in 1859, when it was still called Cherry Creek. In Central City two years later, she turned her home into a hospital, and then the First Methodist Church. "I always go where Jesus calls," she said as she welcomed whites, Native Americans, and fellow African Americans—anyone who needed help.

In 1879, when the first African American families arrived in Kansas to found Nicodemus, they luckily settled near Native American villagers. Lulu Mae Sadler Craig, eleven, recalled

the first grim winter. "The Indians didn't give us any trouble," and they shared their food rations from the government fort.

In 1884, in Cascade, Montana, tall, muscular, former-slave Mary Fields arrived to work at a Catholic

Martin R. Delaney

convent and school for Blackfeet women and girls. She later achieved fame as gun-toting Stagecoach Mary, the second woman in history to deliver the US mail. Gary, a white boy of ten, idolized this mountain of a woman, and years later described her exciting life: "Indians never bothered her because she was a Negro," recalled Gary. (Today Americans know little Gary as Gary Cooper, the Academy Award–winning actor.)

Stagecoach Mary Fields

Throughout the nineteenth-century, leading African American figures rose to defend the rights of indigenous people. Senator Hiram Revels, the first of twenty-two African Americans elected to Congress after the Civil War, was born free in North Carolina of lineage that included African, Irish, and Croatan Indian. A highly educated and well-spoken minister who represented the state of Mississippi, he stood as a symbol of what people of mixed heritage could accomplish with freedom. African American Congressman James O'Hara of North Carolina used his two terms in the House, from 1883 to 1887, to campaign for equal rights for all people of color and also to sponsor a bill to aid the Cherokee Nation.

Perhaps the most stinging public exposure of the US government's genocidal policy toward Native Americans came from B. K. Bruce of Mississippi, a former runaway slave, and the first African American to serve a full six-year Senate term. On April 6, 1880, Bruce rose to tell his Senate colleagues how

US plans and military actions made Native Americans "fugitives and vagabonds in their own land." He summarized:

> "Our Indian policy and administration seem to me to have been inspired and controlled by a stern selfishness, with a few honorable exceptions. Indian treaties have generally been made as the condition and instrument of acquiring the valuable territory occupied by the several Indian nations, and have been changed and revised from time to time as it became desirable that the steadily growing, irrepressible white races should secure more room for their growth and more lands for their occupancy; and war, bounties, and beads have been used . . . for the purpose of temporary peace and security for the whites, and as the preliminary to further aggressions upon the red man's lands, with the ultimate view of his expulsion and extinction from the continent."

The Senator's final plea was to "save and not destroy these people."

This was an era when, in the name of Christianity and civilization, the federal government herded Native Americans onto reservations. Then their children were sent to "Indian schools," where missionaries forced them to "adopt Christian civilization." The African American school, Hampton Normal and Agricultural Institute, opened its doors to a hundred Native Americans. An eager, young ex-slave turned educator, Booker T. Washington, was placed in charge of a project to educate Indians in the ways of white civilization.

In his famous autobiography *Up from Slavery*, Washington described his part in an experiment at Hampton Institute from 1879 to 1881, when he mentored seventy-four Indians youths. "They were like any other human beings," he recalled. "They were continually planning to do something that would add to my happiness and comfort," and Hampton's Black students "tried to help the Indians in every possible way."

When Washington took an Indian student to Washington, D.C., the two found a strange color line. Aboard the steamship, the Native American was admitted to the dining room, and Washington was not. In the nation's capital a hotel manager rented a room to the student, but not to his teacher.

BIRD GEE JOINS "THE HEATHENS"

IN OCTOBER 1875, BIRD Gee, a former runaway slave, dressed in his best Sunday suit, and walked into Mr. Stanley's Kansas inn for a meal. Perhaps he was testing the new civil-rights law passed by Congress and signed by President Grant a few months earlier. Mr. Stanley's waiters told him he, as "a Negro," would not be served. Gee—infuriated by his frustrated plans or angry by the denial of his rights or both—went straight to the US district attorney and demanded his rights under the new law. In April 1876, Mr. Stanley was indicted for a criminal offense. Then followed a protracted legal battle in which Stanley's attorney charged that Congress had no right to make a law governing public accommodations. Finally the case landed in the Supreme Court in 1883 with four others in which African Americans in four states also protested being denied fair treatment despite the new law. One had been denied a seat in the dress circle of a San Francisco theater, another was denied admission to the New York Grand Opera in New York City. Another in Missouri was kept from using hotel facilities, and a Black woman from Tennessee was refused a seat in the "ladies' car" of a train.

The Supreme Court ruled that the new law violated the Constitution, and neither law nor man could keep another man from his American right to discriminate against anyone. The lopsided eight-to-one decision was a clear sign that the three new amendments to the Constitution, and the former slaves they were designed to protect, were being thrown into the dustbin and that the old order was returning in a new form. Loren Miller later wrote with great feeling about how his granduncle Bird Gee decided to leave for the Indian Territory "to spend the rest of his life among the 'heathens' where they was no racial discrimination. He did."

Bird Gee had decided—and with many, many other African Americans—that white society and its laws were not for him, and when he joined the first victims of racism in the Americas, he was pursing a proud tradition.

Loren Miller gained a measure of revenge for his daring granduncle. He became a lawyer, wrote a book about the Supreme Court's treatment of all the Bird Gees in American history, took part in the most prominent civil-rights cases in California, and lived out his last days as a revered judge in the state's superior court.

CONGRESSMAN GEORGE HENRY WHITE

IN THE 1870S, GEORGE Henry White, a former slave of African, Irish, and Native American descent, arrived to attend Whitin

For seven years the Lowry gang, largely Black Indians, fought their own Civil War in North Carolina. First they took on the Confederate Home Guard and then Ku Klux Klan terrorists who used violence and murder to keep their "uppity" people of color "in their place."

Normal School in Lumberton, North Carolina. People in the town were still telling tales about Henry Berry Lowry and his guerilla force, the Lowry gang. As "mixed blood" freemen, they and their families lived in swamps near Lumberton and had no use for the Confederacy or slavery. When the Confederate States Home Guard tried to seize the men and force them to build Confederate fortifications, swamp warfare broke out. After the war, when Lumberton white men joined the Ku Klux Klan, Lowry and his men took on them and even local lawmen. Lowry and his band of people—made up of three races—simply wanted to live free. They spent eight years proving this from their gun barrels.

Young Henry White also decided at an early age to fight for his people and freedom. His weapons were not made of steel, but he was. In 1877 he earned a degree at Howard University, became a teacher and then a principal of a school for African American children. He persuaded a white judge to train him as an attorney, and in 1879 he was admitted to the North Carolina bar.

White turned to politics, was elected to the state's House of Representatives, then the state Senate, then served eight years as a district prosecuting attorney. Tall, strong-willed, and eloquent, White decided to run for Congress from North Carolina's heavily African American 2nd Congressional district. He was elected in 1896 and again in 1898, increasingly gaining white support.

When George Henry White stood to address the 55th and 56th Congresses, he seemed alone. He was the only person of color in either the House or Senate, and his Southern colleagues regaled one another off and on the floor with "darky stories." White became the last former slave to sit in Congress, the last to serve in the nineteenth century, and the first person of color to serve Congress in the twentieth century.

Congressman George Henry White

White reached high office as people of color were stripped of their new Constitutional rights—the right to hold office and to vote and to sit on a jury, testify, or bring suit against a white person in court. Former slaves were becoming debt-ridden and sharecroppers who still labored for their former masters. Many were even worse off—trapped in a convict lease system that convicted them for minor or no crimes, and then exploited their labor, sometimes for decades. Then there was lynch-mob terror that kept people of color "in their place."

White decided violence was not the answer, and he would rely on his education, knowledge, and oratorical skills. He would bring truth to the halls of Congress. Speaking as "the sole representative" of his people, White demanded Constitutional protections for his people. Because he made carefully crafted, hard-hitting speeches, his enraged white foes called him "uppity" and "too damn smart" and chose to ignore him.

Congressman White was a hard man to ignore. In 1900 he infuriated his colleagues when he introduced the country's first federal antilynching bill. He bluntly compared lynching to treason and demanded the death penalty for the convicted. His bill was buried in the judiciary committee and never came to a vote, even though 105 people were lynched that year.

That year, when White rose for his final speech, legislators in North Carolina had made it impossible for him or any other African American to return to the US Congress. White spoke "in behalf of an outraged, heart-broken, bruised, and bleeding, but God-fearing people; faithful, industrious, loyal, rising people—full of potential force." He affirmed his determination: "I am pleading for the life, the liberty, the future happiness, and manhood suffrage for one-eighth of the entire population of the United States." Not until the Great Depression was another African American elected to Congress, and then not from the South but from Chicago.

On January 31, 2011 the mayor and citizens of Tarboro, North Carolina, celebrated native son George Henry White. They dedicated a day to honoring his service to his county, state, and country. A plaque honoring the congressman is displayed on a prominent downtown street, a post office is named after him, and his portrait adorns the county courthouse.

LUCY GONZALEZ PARSONS

LUCY GONZALEZ CHOSE TO battle for justice from outside the system. Born in central Texas in 1853 to a family of African, Native American, and Hispanic ancestry, Lucy Gonzalez had been a slave. In Albert Parsons, a former Confederate soldier, she found a handsome, determined white man who fought bigotry, campaigned for black candidates, and used his hard-hitting newspaper, the *Spectator*, to challenge the KKK. They claimed to have married in Texas, but state law and custom may have made such a marriage illegal.

In the early 1870s, as Klan violence in Texas threatened their lives, the Parsons moved to Chicago. They arrived at the moment laborers, including many immigrants, were forming industrial unions. Radical unionists urged the overthrow of capitalism. Albert and Lucy, self-educated and charismatic, hurled themselves into this turbulent struggle as advocates of a workers' state.

Lucy concentrated on organizing immigrant and other women, writing for radical publications, and speaking at public

Lucy Gonzalez Parsons, born a slave in Texas, fought the KKK and then for equality for women and minorities, and became a major champion of labor unions and socialism. She was a brilliant, self-taught, fiery, radical speaker and writer.

meetings. She urged people to unite across the fiery lines of race, religion, and sex. Justice denied to people of color or women, she insisted, was injustice for all.

Albert became famous as a leading radical organizer, one of the few who was not an immigrant. On May 1, 1886, Lucy,

Albert, and their two young children inaugurated the first May Day parade, leading eighty thousand smiling Chicago workingmen, women, and children along Michigan Avenue. More than a hundred thousand others marched in other US cities.

By then Albert and his allies were targeted for elimination by Chicago's industrial and banking elite. A few days after the peaceful May Day parade, life for the Parsons family changed forever. A labor rally called by Albert became known as the Haymarket Square Riot when seven Chicago policemen died in a bomb blast. No evidence had been found pointing to those who made or detonated the bomb, but Parsons and seven immigrant union leaders were arrested. Urged on by the city's rich and powerful, the media began a patriotic campaign that led to their convictions and death sentences.

Lucy Parsons began a speaking and writing campaign to prove their innocence and to protest their rigged trial and sentences. She seemed to be speaking and leading picket lines everywhere in the state and in the country. But the state of Illinois executed Parsons and three others, anyway, and sent the rest to jail. This delivered a crushing blow to the movement for strong industrial unions that lasted until the 1930s.

Lucy Parsons never ceased her crusade for radical unions, women's rights, and socialism—and to exonerate the Haymarket Martyrs. In 1905 she was one of two women delegates (with two hundred men) who attended the founding convention of the radical Industrial Workers of the World. In one speech she called women "the slaves of slaves" and demanded equal justice.

In a second and longer speech she analyzed the use of strikes. She urged fellow workers "not to strike and go out and starve, but to strike and remain in and take possession of the necessary property of production." She had unfurled a new, nonviolent way to prevent bosses from crushing strikes by importing scab laborers. During the Great Depression of the 1930s, autoworkers effectively used this tactic they called "sit-down strikes."

Others also embraced this new approach. Mahatma Gandhi in India used it against the British, Dr. Martin Luther King Jr. introduced it to the civil-rights movement, and Cesar Chavez and his farm workers also adopted nonviolent resistance. In the late twentieth century, US antiwar movements embraced the tactic, as did hundreds of thousands of people around the world fighting dictators.

One of Lucy Parsons's daring tactics was to march poor women into wealthy Chicago neighborhoods "to confront the rich on their doorsteps." She also spent many a night in American jails. She also toured England to promote unionism and socialism.

Her unrelenting crusade to empower workingmen and women reached far beyond the America of Lucy Parsons. It moved people of many races and languages. In 1942 she died when a fire swept through her Chicago home. Her ideas and heroic example did not die with her.

Despite her fertile mind, oratorical skills, and striking beauty, Lucy Parsons has never appeared in school texts or Hollywood movies. She had four strikes against her: She was born of mixed blood, a slave, a woman, and worked hard all her life. Using what she had, she energetically promoted ideas infuriating to many fellow citizens. Lucy Parsons earned her place in the long fight against economic and political injustices.

THE GREATEST SWEAT AND DIRT
COWBOY WHO EVER LIVED

IMAGINE A WESTERN NOVEL or movie opening with a scene showing black cowboys hard at work on the Texas plains. Since this scene does not square with our traditional picture of the West, we have rarely seen it. Yet thousands upon thousands of African Americans labored on the broad plains of Texas before, during, and after the Civil War. Thousands became cowhands.

Some arrived when Texas was still part of Mexico and took part in the battles that gave birth to the Lone Star Republic. Others came to Texas later, driven by their masters in huge caravans as the Union Army marched through the South. Briefly during the Civil War Texas was a place where slaveholders could safely hide their slaves. Then Texas became free.

The black cowboys remained. "I doubt if Texas has ever seen finer cowboys than those black men," recalled Nan Alverson, whose father had owned slaves near Fort Worth. They had been roping and branding cattle long before they were free.

After the war the average trail crew of eleven that drove cattle up the Chisolm Trail had two or three black men. Eight thousand black cowpunchers helped shape a tradition as American as Thanksgiving and apple pie. For the usual $30 a month and grub they rode the wilderness trails and took their chances with flooding rivers, wild animals, and sudden storms.

They just rarely galloped across the pages of history books or Hollywood and TV movies of the Old West.

COWBOYS AND INDIANS

AS NATIVE AMERICANS FOUGHT their last-ditch battle for survival on the western plains, armed white cowboys symbolized their advancing enemy. The black cowhand with a Stetson hat, leather saddle, and jeans was seen as no less a foe.

Some tried to prove otherwise. Black riders did team up with Indians in various bands. In 1868 a wagon train in Stephens County, Texas, was attacked by an outfit of thirty-one Indians, two Mexicans, and two black men. "Their main leader," reported one white, "was a big negro." In the same region a black man named Cato commanded twenty-five Comanches. When they besieged the Ledbetter Salt Works, Cato was wounded and his raiders driven off.

The next year dozens of Texas citizens near Fort Belknap fought off a large group of Indians commanded by a black man. He issued his orders from a large rock out of rifle range and, after four hours of fighting, ordered his men back with a bugle call. In 1874, in northwestern Texas, a Black Comanche under Quanah Parker, led Kiowas, Cheyenne, Apache, and Comanche against white buffalo hunters.

Jess (right) and his Apache friends

These reports continued to come out of Texas throughout the late 1860s and 1870s. In 1889 a white Texan summarized his frontier experience in these words: "Very frequently runaway negroes would join the Indians and render valuable assistance in stealing and fighting." Even if this Texan exaggerated, he is describing a relationship with Indians that whites on the frontier had.

Nat Love, the only black cowhand to write a full-length autobiography, ran into a Black Indian Nation in 1876 at Yellow Horse Canyon. In his account, he single-handedly battled a dozen native warriors from Yellow Dog's band. Finally, he was knocked unconscious and brought to their village.

They took good care of him, he believed, "because I had proved myself a brave man, and all savages admire a brave man."

He added this description of the nation: "Then Yellow Dog's tribe was composed largely of half-breeds, and there was a large percentage of colored blood in the tribe, and I was a colored man they wanted to keep me, as they thought I was too good a man to die."

Nat Love rode all the western trails convinced Indians were "evil redskins" bent on "terrorizing the settlers . . . defying the government." He accepted the idea that "the only good Indian is a dead Indian." After a fatal shoot-out he and his buddies had with Native Americans, he reported, "we had the satisfaction of knowing we had made several good Indians out of bad ones."

The winds of racial hatred had never stopped and were again swiftly sweeping the land. Few cowhands of any color voiced much concern about white massacres of Indian villages being carried out routinely during these years.

Slavery in the South had been wiped out only to return as segregation and sharecropping. The dark men, women, and children caught in this new southern net also provoked little white concern.

FIGHTING OLD AND NEW INVASIONS

AMONG THE MORE THAN two hundred thousand men of color who fought in the Civil War, some escaped Southern slavery and others fled the Confederate-controlled Indian Territory. As war veterans they expected that their service would be rewarded and the Constitution would protect them. And for a brief time it did. In the former Confederate states, US troops protected African Americans as they voted and were elected to local, state, and federal offices. But by 1877 a grim curtain again descended upon the lives of African Americans in the Southern states.

At about the same time, the US Congress moved against other people of color and of mixed descent. To punish Native American nations who had been forced to aid the Confederacy—and as an excuse to seize Indian lands—the United States moved against Native Americans. Creeks were forced to sell half of their territory for thirty cents an acre. Seminoles had to sell land at fifteen cents an acre. Then, in 1871, Congress decided to sign no more treaties with Native American Nations and instead treat all Indians as "wards of the state." They came under strict federal control and officials, such as US secretary of

This government photograph shows the US Army capture of Natchez, Nano, Victorio, Geronimo and his son, among others, sitting in the front row.

the interior Columbus Delano and his new policy: ". . . [I]t is our duty to coerce" Native Americans into adopting "our habits and customs."

Whites, eager to gain Native American lands in the West, discovered a new way to reach their goal. Between 1872 and 1874 they attacked the huge buffalo herds native people used as a source of food, income, and clothing. Four million buffalo were killed, and hides, which usually sold for thirty dollars each, flooded the market, selling for one dollar a piece. This severe loss drove native people into wandering, poverty, and dependence on federal aid.

After the disputed election of 1876, African Americans lost again. In exchange for control of the White House, a Congress controlled by the Republican party, agreed to withdraw all US troops from the South. This returned all legal power to those who championed white supremacy. It also ended any African American hopes for their Constitutional rights.

That same July the country prepared a massive celebration for its centenary when humiliating news arrived from the West. In late June, Sitting Bull, Crazy Horse, Rain in the Face (who had African ancestry) and two thousand Lakota and Cheyenne fighters surrounded and killed General George Custer and the 266 men of his Seventh Cavalry regiment. This victory stoked the fires of white patriotism and made lives and lands of Native Americans unsafe.

In 1877, as people of color faced a terrifying future, Sitting Bull rose to address his fellow leaders at the Powder River Council. He began by remembering the white foe as "small and feeble when our forefathers first met them, but now great and overbearing.

"Strangely enough, they have a mind to till the soil, and the love of possessions is a disease in them.

"These people have made many rules that the rich may break, but the poor may not! They have a religion in which the poor worship, but the rich will not! They even take tithes of the poor and weak to support the rich and those who rule. They claim this mother of ours, the Earth, for their own use, and fence their neighbors away from her, and deface her with their buildings and their refuse.

"They compel her to produce out of season, and when sterile she is made to take medicine in order to produce again. All this is sacrilege."

Sitting Bull saw disaster, pain, and heartbreak.

> "We cannot dwell side by side. Only seven years ago we made a treaty by which we were assured that the buffalo country should be left to us forever. Now they threaten to take that from us also. My brothers, shall we submit? or shall we say to them: 'First kill me, before you can take possession of my fatherland!'"

As former slaves were reduced to landless peasants working for their former owners in the South, Native American life faced unrelenting assault in the West. President Chester A. Arthur's secretary of the interior announced he would outlaw Native customs deemed "contrary to civilization" and banned traditional ceremonies, dances, and songs. But worse was being planned.

In 1887, Congressman Charles Dawes's General Allotment

Act, also called the Dawes Act, passed Congress—to civilize, Christianize, and reform "savages." Indians, Dawes said, had to "learn selfishness," and this meant "cultivate the ground, live in houses, ride in Studebaker wagons, send children to school, drink whiskey, and own property." Congress struck a lethal blow at centuries of Native American identity, philosophy, religion, culture, and community.

The Dawes Act also ordered the largest American property transfer in history on the claim Native Americans could not take care of their land. A few Native Americans received 160 acres per family, but since few could read and even fewer understood US legal language, these Native Americans briefly became landowners, and then poor and landless peasants the rest of their lives.

In less than half a century, indigenous Americans lost ninety thousand acres of land, two-thirds of what they owned. Ninety thousand people became landless in the country of their ancestors. Millions of acres passed to eager white homesteaders seeking their American dream. But most went to railroad builders, and speculators. Native Americans were economically crushed.

Additionally, the Dawes Act acted against Native American society. In the name of Christian education and assimilation, it carefully sought to destroy family and community life. Children were taken from their parents and sent to schools run by Protestant missionaries. Brother was separated from brother, sister from sister, and then separated from anyone who spoke their language. Speaking a Native language or making contacts that reinforced their Native heritage were severely punished. Far from home, children were thrust into classrooms and instructed in the values of Christianity and private ownership.

To avoid their slipping back to "Indian ways" during summers, pupils were not sent home. They became work apprentices for Christian families who taught them discipline and "civilized values." Abuse was common, unreported, and not corrected.

By 1889, T. J. Morgan, commissioner of Indian Affairs, was pleased to report important progress, including "socialism destroyed" among Native Americans. Morgan issued new demands and threats:

> "The Indians must conform to 'the white man's ways' peaceably if they will, forcibly if they must. They must adjust themselves to their environment and confirm their mode of living substantially to our civilization. . . . They cannot escape it, and must either conform to it or be crushed by it."

During Commissioner Morgan's and the Bureau of Indian Affairs's move to control every aspect of Native American life, the white South moved to solve its "racial problem." Each Southern state enacted laws that denied African Americans the right to vote, hold office, serve on juries, or exercise any rights of citizenship. Life for African Americans was marked by segregation, discrimination, and the terror of lynching.

In 1936 the federal government admitted its US Indian agents (paid only one thousand dollars a year) had used the Dawes Act for theft and personal enrichment. Hardly mentioned was how Congress undermined indigenous nations and families, and stripped Native Americans of their lands. It took another generation before the United States acknowledged the damages, including the economic ones, inflicted upon African American families by state racial laws. Unmentioned was the fact that each US administration, without exception, did not enforce the new Constitutional amendments that promised all "a new birth of freedom."

THE BUFFALO SOLDIERS

AFTER THE CIVIL WAR, US policy was brought forcefully home to Native Americans on the bayonets of US infantry and cavalry regiments assigned to the frontier. For the first time, officially, this included black men, the Ninth and Tenth Cavalry and the Twenty-fourth and Twenty-fifth Infantry Regiments, "US Colored Troops."

There is a painful irony that these intrepid black soldiers took part in the final defeat of Native Americans, the first victims of racism in the Americas. But take part they did in the last Indian wars. Because their short curly hair was similar to that on the buffalo's neck, Indians called them "buffalo soldiers," and the name stuck. They marched forth to carry out the orders of their white officers and their government in Washington whose policies made peace impossible.

As the buffalo soldiers dutifully brought a white version of law and order to the frontier, they earned the respect of every military friend and foe they encountered. They guarded railroad and telegraph lines, stagecoaches and arms shipments, towns and homesteads, whites and Indians.

They moved Indian families and nations from one location to another and rode after those who left reservations to seek some freedom or merely to forage for food for starving people. From the Canadian border to the Rio Grande, from St. Louis to the Rockies and into California, the buffalo soldiers rolled up an impressive record.

Their desertion rate was the lowest in the frontier army though their posts were often in the most remote, Godforsaken places. This was a time when more than a third of white enlisted men went A.W.O.L. each year. In 1876, for example, the white Seventh Cavalry had 72 deserters, the Third had 170, and the Fifth had 224, but the black Ninth only had 6 deserters and the Tenth 18.

As black men in a white man's army, they were subject to unusually harsh discipline, bigoted officers, and poor food and recreational facilities. The Tenth regimental standard was home-made, tattered, and worn—unlike the silk-embroidered banner supplied by headquarters to white units.

Yet often their morale was high and some white officers were proud to lead so brave a military force. For scouts they had such frontier legends as Kit Carson, Wild Bill Hickok, and the Seminole Negro Indian Scouts.

Black troopers, including those with Black Indian ancestry, operated under orders that often had them viewing Native Americans through the gunsights of their ready carbines. Eleven black soldiers earned the Congressional Medal of Honor in combat against Utes, Apaches, Comanches. The first of the eleven, Corporal Emmanuel Stance, a short ex-slave serving in Company F, Ninth Cavalry, had five encounters with Plains Nations in two years. He behaved with such valor and calmness that he won unstinting praise from his white commander along with his country's highest military decoration.

Arist Frederic Remington sketched a meeting in the West between a Plains Indian and a Buffalo Soldier in his Sign Language.

THE SIGN LANGUAGE.

In an age that offered black men few decent, manly jobs, military life appealed to the recruits. Many had served their country during the Civil War. There is evidence that some men disagreed with their government's genocidal policies toward Native Americans. But they certainly carried out orders.

Artist Frederic Remington, who traveled with the Tenth Cavalry in Arizona, found them "charming men with whom to serve." He also reported to a white reading public that thought of blacks as meek, fearful, clownish people, that they were truly fearless, determined, and willing killers.

George Washington Williams was one buffalo soldier appalled by the injustice and oppression of Native Americans. At fourteen he lied about his age so he could fight in the Civil War. In 1868 he joined Mexico's effort to overthrow Emperor Maximilian, its French colonial tyrant. On his first day on the prairie, Sergeant Major Williams wrote of his fellow Tenth Cavalrymen: "We remembered of having read . . . that it is wrong to persecute the poor Indian, that he owned the whole country; that the 'white people would have to answer for their wickedness in the *Day of Judgment.*'" When Williams found he was serving under a white officer who said he was "thirsting for Indian blood," he decided "killing people isn't a job for a Christian." He left the army. In 1881 wrote the century's most important history of African Americans.

We do not know how many other men like Williams served as buffalo soldiers, but we do know that in 1879, when Texas Rangers rode toward a Kiowa village seeking scalps, they were intercepted by Tenth Cavalrymen. And in 1887, Ninth Cavalrymen turned back Colorado militiamen who planned to attack a Ute reservation.

Buffalo soldiers lived through adventures rich in irony. They never knew when they might be ambushed not just by the foes they faced in the field, but by the white townspeople they protected. For merely entering some towns or saloons, particularly in Texas, they became embroiled in shoot-outs or became targets for cowardly snipers.

One Texas citizen murdered a black trooper, killed the two black cavalrymen who came to arrest him, and then was found not guilty by a jury of his white peers. At times animosity toward bluecoats in Texas was so vicious that black and white US soldiers united to defend themselves from those they were guarding. Soldiering had lost its Civil War glamour and had not yet picked up its Hollywood frontier-movie, patriotic gloss.

In 1890 black troopers were summoned to assist in the suppression of the last Indian uprising, the Ghost Dance Rebellion. Really a Sioux religious revival and prayer for survival, it managed to terrify local whites.

The US Army command ordered in its troops. After surrounding the Sioux at Wounded Knee, the Seventh Cavalry opened fire on 350 innocent men, women, and children. One of the fifty survivors of the massacre recalled, "We tried to run but they shot us like we were buffalo."

Black troops were not involved in the slaughter, but the Ninth Cavalry had been assigned to herding the Ghost Dancers together. To celebrate their part in the action, a Ninth Cavalry cavalryman wrote a ballad that ended with the lines:

> The Red Skins heard the Ninth was near
> And fled in great dismay.

The ironic nature of the black military legacy on the frontier was sharply etched in the life and death of Isaiah Dorman, a Black Sioux, who fought and died with General George Custer at the Little Big Horn.

Dorman had worked for the army for many years and was considered "faithful and reliable in every trust." He was fluent in Sioux languages, married to a Santee Sioux woman, and had become good friends with Chief Sitting Bull. And there he was riding with Custer toward the Little Big Horn and immortality on June 25, 1876.

When the Seventh Cavalry plunged into the trap, a badly wounded Dorman survived the battle. Sitting Bull reportedly approached the wounded Black Sioux and said to his men, "Don't kill that man, he's a friend of mine." Sitting Bull gave Dorman a drink of water from his buffalo horn, and then Dorman died.

⇥ ⇤

WHITE FRONTIERSMAN ANDREW DAVIS wrote, "It was believed that Indians never killed Negroes—that the worst they did to them was to take them prisoner. It was not often they did that." His optimistic view is not consistent with the facts. Members of the two races did shoot and kill each other, and African Americans were captured by Native Americans.

But his words highlight a basic truth—there was something very different in the relationship between the two dark races, than the one either had with whites. However, life on the last frontier could be violent and short for anyone.

Evidence of this Old West Black Indian relationship is preserved in frontier documents and captured in the flash of the camera's eye. This startling new device had arrived in the West by the 1870s and 1880s—with its puff of white smoke—to capture westerners in frozen frames for all time.

OUR BLACK INDIAN TALE of the last frontier nears its end with five people seeking something they considered vital to their lives. Britton Johnson was searching for his kidnapped family. Isom Dart was seeking his love. Jim and Kitty Cloud Taylor sought each other and the happiness of marriage. Bill Pickett was trying to develop his cowhand skills so he could feed his large family.

Britton Johnson's fascinating saga began before the Civil War when "Brit" was known as one of the best shots on the Texas frontier. He was described as "a shining jet black negro of splendid physique" and lived with his wife and four children in a white settlement in Young County, Texas.

In October 1864, when Johnson may still have been a slave, Comanche and Kiowa men besieged his settlement. They killed some people, including his son, and galloped off with several women and children, including his wife and his three other children. Johnson persuaded his fellow villagers that he could bring the prisoners back, and he set off alone on this mission.

One story holds that he entered an Indian village and then helped the prisoners to escape. Another story states that Johnson negotiated with the Kiowas and Comanches to win their release, and this was a long and complicated process.

Matthew Braun, a western novelist, tells this story in *Black Fox*, in words he claims are "essentially true and accurate in detail." Braun takes the brave black man through a series of harrowing contests and encounters that he finally convinced the Kiowas and Comanches to release their captives to Johnson in exchange for horses and ponies. It is a rousing, well-told yarn and restores to this unsung hero, states Braun, "his audacity and fearlessness . . . as real as any to emerge from Western folklore."

Unfortunately for Johnson, this was not his last perilous encounter with Plains Nations. In January 1871, Johnson and three other black cowpunchers were hauling supplies on the Butterfield Trail to the Johnson family home near Fort Griffin. Suddenly twenty-five Comanches rode into view and a sharp gunfight on the broad plains soon became a life-and-death struggle.

Brit Johnson took charge of the cowhands' defense, ordering them to kill their horses and use their bodies for breastworks. The Comanches charged again and again, firing and riding toward and over the men sprawled out behind their horses. The bitter battle finally took the life of every cowhand but Johnson. He gathered up the rifles of his fallen buddies, quickly loaded them, and poured a steady fire into the attackers.

But this time Johnson's cunning, accuracy, and courage were not enough. He had fired 173 shots—the number of empty cartridges found near him—when he was cut down by enemy bullets. Possibly infuriated it took so long to slay their opponent, the Indians mutilated his body and killed his dog. "A man of heroic qualities," said one of his neighbors, had died.

Not death but love and violence entered the life of famed black cattle rustler Isom Dart in the person of an attractive Shoshone woman named Tickup and her daughter Mincy, nine. Amiable, likable Dart thought it was love at first sight, and he took in the pair who were fleeing Tickup's violent Ute husband, Pony Beater. He drank a lot, beat up his wife and her daughter and then fell asleep. When he had done that once too often the two escaped.

Dart, with the two under his protection, left to avoid a confrontation with the enraged husband. But Pony Beater tracked them down and caught them by surprise. He had Tickup bind Dart with leather thongs and then took off with his family and Dart's possessions.

The first night on the trail Pony Beater drank, beat up mother and daughter, and dropped off to sleep. He never woke up. Tickup slit his throat, gathered up Mincy, and headed back home to Idaho. There she hoped to find some peace.

Meanwhile Dart freed himself and tracked down his new family. He arrived in Idaho to find Tickup already had chosen a new Indian husband. Enraged, he charged at and was about to murder the man when Tickup, ever resourceful, clobbered Dart with a stone axe so hard she almost severed his ear.

Dart decided romance was not for him and returned to Brown's Park, Colorado, and a rustler's life. He became "the best bronco

rider who ever threw a leg over a horse," according to one friend. He also became a target for bounty hunter Tom Horn. At the age of fifty-one Dart was shot in the back by Horn for the reward.

Compared with Dart, John Taylor was far more successful with life, love, and Ute Indians. His story appears in three frontier photographs. The first shows Taylor proudly posing with a Ute friend. The next shows Taylor on his wedding day in 1894 when he married Kitty Cloud of the Ute Nation. Taylor is on the ground in his wedding suit, Utes to the right and left of him with spears and rifles poised at his heart. It looks as though Taylor is about to die. The photograph captures a menacing moment.

But a closer look reveals that Taylor is lying on a blanket Even his neat white hat rests on the blanket. This is clearly a posed photograph. Everyone is having some fun making it seem John Taylor is about to leave this earth at the hands of the Utes.

The last photograph shows Kitty Cloud Taylor, her sister, and their babies. It is clear that Mrs. Taylor's child has African

Kitty Cloud Taylor and her child (right), with her sister and sister's child (left)

as well as Ute features. The three pictures add up to a tale of love, marriage, and family. They also personalize a long racial friendship being continued by two people in love.

"THE BULL DOGGER"

IN MANY WAYS THE exciting saga of Bill Pickett tells us what happened to Black Indians as the last frontier entered the twentieth century. Pickett was born in 1870, the second of thirteen children, to Black Cherokees in Oklahoma.

After completing the fifth grade, Pickett left the dull confines of a frontier classroom for the wild life of the range. He landed a job as a ranch hand and developed his roping and riding skills. But Bill Pickett wanted something more of life.

He found it among the animals he tended. Some people say that when he was only ten, Pickett began to practice a technique for holding calves quiet at branding time. Others say he began his startling skill later in Texas brush country where roping a steer was difficult if not impossible. What Pickett did was to create a cowhand technique for holding cattle that required delicate coordination, great strength, and pure macho guts.

It is called "bulldogging" or "steer-wrestling" and became the most famous cowboy sport. Pickett would race his horse Spradley after a steer and leap out of the saddle onto the animal's back. Grabbing a horn in each hand, he began the hard part. He twisted the horns until the beast's face turned upward and the huge animal fell over on its side. Rider and steer skidded to a halt in a cloud of dust.

For a final touch, Pickett sunk his teeth into the steer's upper lip or nose and let go with his hands. The startled beast lay still, shocked someone was biting its nose or lip. Everyone watching was amazed that the cowhand's only grip on the big

John Taylor on his wedding day

animal was white teeth clamped onto a lip or nose.

Pickett had a wife and eventually nine children to feed. To provide for his family, he landed a job with the huge 101 Ranch in Oklahoma run by the Miller brothers. Zack Miller hired the two hundred best cowhands he could find for his ranch and rodeo. His men won so many prizes they were soon barred from local cowboy competition.

Miller took his rodeo on the road, and they performed and entertained in Mexico City, London, New York, and in Argentina and Canada. Everywhere their featured act was Bill Pickett's bull-dogging. Billed as the "Dusky Demon" or the "Wonderful Colored Cowboy," Pickett's daring act drew the applause and admiration of young and old, cowboy and city slicker.

Pickett's five foot six, 145-pound frame swept through his bulldogging feat with the agility of a ballet dancer. He never appeared to get scratched. His other ranching talents were such that Zack Miller called Pickett "the greatest sweat and dirt cowboy that ever lived, bar none." That lofty title may still hold.

At one time or another in his rodeo career Pickett had the assistance of two other 101 cowhands destined to win fame and fortune—Tom Mix and Will Rogers. Back then they were just beginners who assisted the Dusky Demon in his famous act.

In his later years Pickett made two silent films. One was a black cowhand mystery movie. The other, called *The Bull-Dogger,* demonstrated his steer-wrestling artistry. Sadly, no copy of either has been found.

Pickett died in 1932, after a stallion he had tried to rope while on foot turned on him. From coast to coast he was remembered, and in New York comedian and actor Will Rogers wrote to the *New York Times* about his brave buddy. He told how Pickett had

Bill Pickett

created a sport that brought ranch and cowpuncher life to millions of people who had never been out West.

Pickett's enduring legacy is that he single-handedly invented a sport as challenging and rough as the American outdoors. He demonstrated that one man with courage and stamina can

Poster for Bill Pickett movie

overcome a dangerous beast.

Aboard his favorite horse, Spradley, Bill Pickett rode into the twentieth century. He had invented and mastered a perilous technique for handling steers and turned his creation into a rodeo performance. He loped in casually, as was his style, wearing his talents like comfortable western jeans. He appeared to perform his miraculous act effortlessly.

Bill Pickett's life brings our story of Black Indians to a close. He began life in the nineteenth century as a ranch hand with a large family to feed, and ended up in the twentieth as a talented cowhand and cherished performer.

With his masterful skills, Pickett won fame and a decent living. But he never achieved in his lifetime the renown and riches of his two assistants, Tom Mix and Will Rogers. He made a journey from rural to urban life, and counted on a white world for his livelihood. It offered even Bill Pickett limited opportunities.

The 101 Ranch Rodeo in 1914. Bill Pickett, the featured act, sits third from the right in a white shirt. The next white shirted person to the left is Will Rogers, and to his left is Tom Mix. Pickett taught both men some tricks.

SO LONG TO ARTICULATE

THE PUEBLO REVOLT

DURING A MAY 2009 visit to Santa Fe, which was eagerly preparing to celebrate its four hundredth anniversary, I met the official planners of the event. I also met with the executive board of the NAACP and representatives of Native American cultural organizations. I learned that the white organizers were planning a celebration when local people of color persuaded them it should also be a commemoration. I accidentally learned even more one day as I sat in a small Santa Fe park waiting for the Native American Art Museum across the street to open.

The park's statue and plaque celebrated a leading figure in the 1680 Pueblo revolt that overthrew Spanish colonial rule. This revolt was no minor event for the city, the southwest, and Spain's claims in North America. As Spanish conquistadores penetrated the southwest, enslaved Africans among them escaped whenever they could. The Navaho, Apache, Ute, and the western Pueblo—which included Hopi and Zuni Nations—welcomed those who deserted the conquerors, and found Africans had much to offer.

Resentment grew in the southwest as Spain's missionaries undermined Pueblo culture, and its officials ordered the execution of Pueblo priests. In 1650 and 1667, Pueblo villages erupted in violence. Then in 1675, Spain provoked a crisis with a public hanging of three Pueblo priests and whipping forty-three others. One of those whipped was Popé, an elderly Tewa and charismatic medicine man devoted to his people. He also proved to be a master of military tactics. With a small band of officers he planned a broad-based, massive rising.

In a sacred room at Taos, Popé and his commanders spent five years plotting to overthrow Spanish rule, end Christianity, and return to ancient ways. One of his African commanders was Domingo Naranjo, described as "very tall, black with very large, yellow eyes." Their recruits, seventeen thousand fighters from dozens of villages spread over more than hundreds of miles, included young men like Naranjo who were born of African-Pueblo marriages. Since his troops spoke six different languages and many dialects, Popé's officers created a unique communication system based on tying knots in ropes.

In August 1680 a thousand soldiers bearing muskets, swords, and knives launched Popé's Revolt and were followed by unarmed men ready to seize arms from fallen Europeans. Spanish missionaries, settlers, and soldiers fled to Santa Fe with stories of burning homes, murdered ranch families, and fields set afire. Jubilant rebels surrounded Santa Fe—some on horses, others on foot, many waving weapons, dancing exuberantly, and yelling defiance.

Although Spanish governor Antonio de Otermín claimed Pueblo forces "burned the holy temple and many houses," Popé opposed massacres, and his field commanders rejected random violence. The rebels generously granted thousands of Spaniards safe passage from Santa Fe.

Once in control of the region, Popé's forces took careful aim at Christian symbols. Pueblos marched from village to village destroying Christian religious and cultural artifacts. They killed twenty-one of thirty-three priests, set fire to churches, and buried holy icons in manure. Pueblo families renounced their baptismal names and some leaped into streams to wash away Christian holy oils. Farmers promised not to grow European crops. A document by Commander Naranjo revealed how Popé instructed villagers to "break the lands and enlarge their cultivated fields . . . [as] in ancient times. He said that this is the legitimate cause and the reason they had for rebelling. . . . They had always desired to live as they had. . . ."

The Revolt of 1680 led to years of Pueblo self-rule. But then Popé died, and his followers were crushed by Spain's troops and native allies.

The statue and plaque (erected in 1956) in the park did not celebrate Popé, Commander Naranjo, other Pueblo officers, nor even the July Fourth nature of this stunning victory for liberty and self-determination. It celebrated New Mexico governor Diego de Vargas. The plaque described Vargas as "a devout Christian with a strong devotion to Nuestra Señora, La Conquistadora, Our Lady of Peace." It praised his "accomplishments," "competency and talent," and his "remarkable reconciliation with Pueblo Indian leaders" that "forged a lasting peace that has endured for more than three hundred years."

Governor Vargas undoubtedly played a crucial role during those years. But *The Journals of don Diego de Vargas* reveals a

This statue and park in Santa Fe memorializes Spanish governor and military leader Diego de Vargas, who played a crucial role in the famous Pueblo Revolt of 1680, which he violently overthrew.

different person and story. In 1692, Vargas led the Spanish armies that overthrew the Pueblo revolt. He ordered the execution of seventy leaders and sentenced four hundred men and women to slavery. Then he initiated his own dictatorship. In 1696 fourteen Pueblo villages united again, this time to overthrow their new tyrant. Governor Vargas again prevailed and conducted a deadly retribution one historian has described as "unmerciful, thorough and prolonged."

Governor Diego de Vargas deserves recognition only if our American standard is unremittingly violent, ruthless, and systematic opposition to the ideals of Patrick Henry, Thomas Jefferson, and Ben Franklin. If a twenty-first-century democracy still celebrates men who battled those who bravely sought freedom and justice, new thinking is needed. When monuments, schools, and textbooks heap admiring words on a long dead and dishonored slaveholding elite or Indian-fighting class, children are being taught the wrong lessons.

When I met with planners of Santa Fe's four hundredth anniversary, they had begun to learn about Popé's Revolt from local Native Americans who wanted his story honestly told. They were being told the Santa Fe celebration also needed a commemoration. I then told them the story of the little known Black Indian woman who traveled to Santa Fe eighty years prior to the Pueblo revolt. Before she left Mexico City—the capital of New Spain on January 8, 1600—Isabel de Olvera dictated a demand for her safety. De Olvera appeared before a town mayor who agreed to sign her declaration of protection. "I have some reason to fear that I may be annoyed by some individual since I am a mulatto. It is proper to protect my rights in such an eventuality by an affidavit showing that I am a free woman, unmarried and the legitimate daughter of Hernando, a Negro, and an Indian named Magdalena . . . I demand justice." Her document is the first known protest by an American who was a Native American, African American, and Black Indian woman. Her "I demand justice" preceded the Mayflower Compact by a generation and July Fourth by more than a century and a half. Isabel de Olvera has something to teach us.

Africans sailed with Columbus and other European expeditions to the Americas, and some of the earliest were hired as translators.

Back east I also found white people who heard little about the historic relationship between Africans and Native Americans. They knew by the early nineteenth century, slave ships had brought millions of Africans here. But they did not know Africans who accompanied the earliest European expeditions did not come in chains, but as free people. They were translators for European explorers and merchants and rose to play vital roles as negotiators and diplomats with Native Americans.

Before Columbus, Prince Henry the Navigator of Portugal sent crews of sailors along Africa's Atlantic coast, where they encountered people who spoke many different tongues. Some had extraordinary language skills. In 1453, Prince Henry ordered African interpreters hired on his voyages of discovery to act as translators with the Native Americans. Very soon after, Spain, Holland, France, and England also began to rely on African translators in the Americas. "Especially in the earliest contact period, Africans were highly valued by Europeans as interpreters with the Native Americans," explained historian Peter Bakker. "These men of African origins were not slaves but free black men in the employ of various European trading and exploratory ventures."

Historian Ira Berlin described how African translators he called "Atlantic Creoles" built solid trade relations with Native Americans. They were, Berlin wrote admiringly, "fluent in new languages, and intimate with its trade and cultures, they were cosmopolitan in the fullest sense." In North America, historian J. Leitch Wright Jr. confirmed "both whites and Indians relied heavily on Negro interpreters."

My fellow New Yorkers know that in 1609, Henry Hudson reached what Native Americans called Manhattes, the Dutch called New Amsterdam, and today we call Manhattan. But few knew that around the time of Hudson's landing, French and Dutch ship captains were using African interpreters when trading with Native Americans. An African named Mathieu da Costa served the French in Canada and may have visited Manhattes between 1607 and 1609. In 1612, Dutch merchant Thijs Mossel built a wooden trading post at 45 Broadway, so his African interpreter, Jan Rodriguez, could trade with Native Americans. A year later Mossel and another Dutch employer were locked in a court battle over who had legal right to Rodriguez's knowledge and skills.

Historian Peter Wood described Timboe in South Carolina in 1710 as a "highly valued" African interpreter among Native Americans and called his role "emblematic of the intriguing [African] intermediary position" in the Americas. Some translators began to climb the ladder from interpreter to negotiator to diplomat. By 1650, Atlantic Creoles had built thriving communities in Havana, Mexico City, and San Salvador. Like Isobel de Olivera, these early pioneers have something to teach us.

THE PAST AND ITS FUTURE

SINCE 1968, WHEN DR. Marin Luther King Jr. mobilized a Poor People's March that invited whites and people of color—African Americans and Native Americans to Puerto Ricans, Asian-Americans and Mexican-Americans—mixed-race people have begun to receive a long delayed recognition. King, whose own ancestors included Native Americans as well as Africans, was assassinated in Memphis before the March reached Washington, and its tent city soon sank into the Washington mud. But King's effort had gained support from union leader Ceasar

Chavez, Native Americans Clyde Bellecourt and Dennis Banks, and two hundred members of the National Indian Youth Council. He had broken a barrier in modern interracial relations. That same year Black comedian and activist Dick Gregory went to jail in Olympia, Washington, for defending Native American fishing rights two years before. These actions announced, from one end of the country to the other, that a Black Indian alliance was still alive.

The American Indian Movement (AIM) inspired by King, Gregory, civil-rights marchers, and particularly the Black Power Movement, and born in that crucial year of 1968, also mobilized to redress grievances. AIM members undertook a series of dramatic nonviolent protests beginning in 1969, when its members occupied Alcatraz Island for nineteen months. In 1970, AIM seized a replica of the *Mayflower* on Thanksgiving Day and also occupied iconic Mount Rushmore. In 1971, Native Americans occupied the Bureau of Indian Affairs building in Washington. In 1972 the movement conducted a Trail of Broken Treaties. In 1973, Dennis Banks, Russell Means, and other AIM members occupied the Pine Ridge Indian Reservation, site of the US Seventh Cavalry's infamous 1890 massacre of Lakota villagers at Wounded Knee.

By 1995, Reverend Louis Farrakhan's Million Man March featured Native American, as well as African American speakers who focused on issues important to peoples of color. From their prison cells Mumia Abu-Jamal and Leonard Peltier repeatedly spoke in support of each other as fellow political prisoners.

By the first decade of the new twenty-first century, Harry Belafonte, Danny Glover, and other African American figures, some with Native American roots, had joined the struggle for

Native American rights. Recently the Smithsonian Institution mounted a traveling exhibit "The First and the Forced," which emphasized the historic link between Native Americans and African Americans.

CONFRONTING A TANGLED HISTORY

PEOPLE OF COLOR SHARE the experience of genocide, brutality, exploitation, colonization, and marginalization. But they also have "tangled histories" that make alliances slippery. Often they have had to overcome sharp differences stemming from the nature, timing or characteristics of their oppression, and who ordered and who inflicted the wounds. Divide and rule flourished when European colonizers, white enslavers, and a white Congress, president, and court system set the rules and issued orders. Many times a powerful white society was able to pit one people of color against another, and since 1492 this has been a goal. Divide and rule marked the colonial era. Some Native Americans accepted bribes to hunt African runaways, and some African Americans were enlisted to fight Indians. There is also a larger story: that of the many who refused to fight, that needs a more thorough telling.

Noted Native American scholar Vine Deloria Jr. has described red and black people as having walked noble journeys on separate roads and only sometimes marching on parallel paths. After the Civil War, African American citizenship rights were written into the Constitution, but not for Native Americans nor for women. In World War II the US Army inducted Native Americans into "white units," but kept African Americans (and Japanese Americans) in segregated units.

Various kinds of subjugation and cruelty stir different responses and acts of resistance. Unlike African Americans, Native Americans did not seek to integrate into a dominant society or to assimilate with whites. "Blacks seemed to be saying that white society was bad, but they wanted it anyway," Deloria wrote.

Many Native Americans claim their primary fight is for land and self-identity. Some even view their tortured confinement and painful separation on reservations as at least preserving their cultural integrity. Native Americans more often prefer to identify not with King but with Stokley Carmichael and Malcolm X (who built a Black Power Movement promoting separation from white society). "We only wondered why it had taken so long to articulate. . . ." said Deloria.

The growing interest in the Black Indian story has yet to eradicate centuries of educational neglect, racial division, and animosity. The election of a US president with an African father—and a wife with African and Native American lineage—has helped highlight the role of multiracial people. So has the recent rise of indigenous and Black Indian presidents in Latin America. But schools, texts, and the media in the United States have only timorously begun to examine this heritage. They are slow to embrace its honorable if turbulent past.

Recent events point to distances still to be traveled. Marilyn Vann, president of the Descendants of Freedmen of the Five Tribes, and attorneys for her organization, are currently assisting in two court cases of discrimination against African-descended people by leaders of Native American Nations. (Full disclosure: I have served as a consultant for Ms. Vann's legal team.) Leaders of the Seminole Nation (since 2000) and of the Cherokees (since 2003) have tried to legally exclude members with African descent from citizenship, participation, and government benefits, despite the 1866 treaty with the United States that protected the rights of these members. Seminole and Cherokee leaders have made no effort to exclude members who are also of European lineage.

They invoke the right of sovereignty, a vital issue for Native American Nations living under a powerful United States. Dr. Jack D. Forbes, a Powhatan-Renape-Cherokee and the leading Native American authority on the relationships between Africans and Native Americans, affirmed the crucial importance of sovereignty. But he pointed out that sovereignty should not trump justice, history, or simple fairness. Dr. Forbes stated that sovereignty, for example, does not allow New Jersey, New Mexico, or any other state to legally discriminate against its citizens because of their race, color, religion, or anything else.

The disheartening efforts of the Cherokee and Seminole leaders demonstrate the durability of the divisive racial doctrines Europeans planted over five hundred years ago. They still support white superiority and divide peoples of color.

Half a century ago Vine Deloria Jr. wrote in his *Custer Died for Your Sins: An Indian Manifesto*:

> [T]he understanding of the racial question does not ultimately involve understanding by either blacks or Indians. It involves the white man himself. He must examine his past. He must face the problems he has created within himself and within others. The white man must no longer project his fears and insecurities onto other groups, race, and countries. Before the white man can relate to others he must forego the pleasure of defining them.

THE PERSONAL SOJOURN THAT led to a book named *Black Indians* began in the 1930s and with my father, Ben Katz, who fell in love with African American blues and jazz music. He first had a large 78-rpm record collection, and then a large collection of African American history books and pictures. I had to be one of the few white kids who went to bed listening to Bessie Smith, Sidney Bechet, and Louis Armstrong, and woke up surrounded by the writings of Frederick Douglass, W. E. B. Du Bois, and E. Franklin Frazier. At a very early age Dad took me to Harlem's Schomburg Center for Research in Black Culture, which he considered sacred ground. He also organized jazz concert benefits for the United Negro and Allied War Veterans of America, so I met Sidney Bechet and James P. Johnson in our living room. Bunk Johnson sat at our table at the Stuyvesant Casino. Mezz Mezzcrow introduced me to Louis Armstrong after his Carnegie Hall concert. I also began to fall in love with jazz, blues, and this history.

Dad helped found the Committee for the Negro in the Arts with Charles White, Frank Silvera, Ernie Crichlow, and Walter Christmas. Walter and Ernie became Dad's best friends, and I got to meet stimulating men and women of color. Before I joined the US Navy in 1945, my senior high-school thesis was a two-hundred-page history of jazz—best described as amateurish, emotional, and well illustrated.

My fourteen years as a New York public school teacher were spent "bootlegging" my new knowledge into my social studies classrooms, to offset the appalling omissions and distortions of the state curriculum and its approved textbooks. By 1967 a small

New York publisher agreed to issue my *Eyewitness*, a Black history text I developed in my classes. I had written to Langston Hughes asking for permission to use several of his articles, and one evening in late 1966 my phone rang. "What kind of book is it?" he asked. I explained it was a Black history book for young people and schools. His response was immediate and firm. "Don't leave out the cowboys!" I think he said it twice.

"Yes, I have two chapters on them," I said.

"Good, good," he said. "That's very important." I had his permission.

But I had something more. His five words changed my life. I knew the great poet of urban America had grown up in Lawrence, Kansas, and was named after his great-uncle, John Mercer Langston, a frontier lawyer who defended Underground Railroad agents, including his brother, Charles Langston in Ohio. Another ancestor was Lewis Sheridan Leary, an Oberlin College student who fought and died with John Brown at Harpers Ferry. Langston Hughes also could trace his ancestry back to Pocahontas. My eyes were opening to a new kind of frontier.

I also had become familiar with the pioneering

Black Indian attorney and Congressman John Mercer Langston

research on Africans and Indians on America's frontiers by Kenneth Wiggins Porter, a white Harvard-trained university professor. In 1968, when a *New York Times* company asked me to serve as general editor of 212 African American reprint classics, I had Porter select his best essays for his *The Negro on the American Frontier*. It appeared in 1971, as did my *The Black West: A Documentary and Pictorial History of the African American Role in the Westward Expansion of the United States*. After Professor Porter's death in 1981, his wife made me curator of his unpublished manuscripts, and I quickly found them a home at Harlem's Schomburg Center.

Meanwhile faces of Black Indians—Apaches, Kiowa, Cherokees, Seminoles, and others—peered from the antique photographs I had selected for *The Black West*. I was looking at America's first Freedom Fighters, our first Underground Railroad conductors, and our country's first Rainbow Coalition. My proposal for a book on Black Indians brought a single publisher response: Atheneum's young adult editor Marcia Marshall.

Rules of the day for young adult books had advantages: It had to be written clearly and informally, use illustrations, explain important concepts, minimize "scholarship," omit footnotes, and remain less than two hundred pages. These also proved to be disadvantages. Many readers of *Black Indians* wanted more evidence, scholarship, and deeper coverage—more than the less than two hundred pages could provide. Then there were US boards of education limitations, such as minor coverage of Latin America. The final product bent a few rules by using many original sources, historical engravings and photographs as evidence, and provided more on Latin America than usual.

I am pleased for the opportunity afforded by this new and

expanded edition, to improve on the original effort by offering far more information, documentation, visual evidence, and to introduce many more daring Americans of color.

In this 1990 photo from Word Up *magazine, LL Cool J holds up his copy of* Black Indians *to affirm his mixed ancestry.*

ACKNOWLEDGMENTS TO THE REVISED EDITION

THIS PROJECT GREW FROM a lingering fascination with the pioneer research that was begun by Professor Kenneth Wiggins Porter when Herbert Hoover sat as our Great White Father in the White House. As an editor for Arno Press/*New York Times*, I was able to have Professor Porter select his best articles for and edit *The Negro on the American Frontier* (1971). After some minor skirmishes with the subject in my *The Black West* (1971) and *Black People Who Made the Old West* (1977) in 1977, I also tried to summarize some Black Indian history in a short *Freedomways* article. After Professor Porter's death in July 1981, Mrs. Annette Porter made me curator of her husband's uncompleted manuscripts (housed at the Schomburg Center for Black Culture in New York City) and my interest mounted.

Along the way I have benefited enormously from research offered by Dr. Joseph Opala, who shared valuable data with me on the African Seminoles; work with Professor Earl Davis, formerly of New York University's African American Studies Center; Marcia White, who had worked with the American Museum of Natural History in New York City; and (as always) the late Sara Dunlop Jackson of the National Archives in Washington, D.C.; and by discussions with Dr. John Hope Franklin, and Ernest Kaiser of the Schomburg Center for Research in Black Culture, William Miles, Charles Fuller, Jean Carey Bond, George Tooks, Warren Halliburton, Tony Brown, Esther and James Jackson, and Charlayne Haynes.

The direct impetus for this volume came from challenging discussions with audiences at three lively forums provided by Marcia White at New York's American Museum of Natural History. Here was a case of a lecturer learning more from the audience than they learned from him. Thank you, Marcia White and audiences.

My researchers included Rosalee Hamilton and Erika Lieber, and my patient proofreader of the original edition was Laurie Lehman.

This revised edition greatly benefited from critical exchanges with many of the names mentioned above; as well as from Pompey Fixico of the Wild Cat John Horse Band, Rose Davis of *Indian Voices*, and Taino leader Roberto Borrero; Dr. Ivan and Dr. Jacqui Van Sertima; Dr. John Hope Franklin; Howard Zinn; thousands of readers and listeners here and abroad; audiences on both sides of the Atlantic; and my long talkative marriage to Dr. Laurie Lehman.

BIBLIOGRAPHY

Ashbaugh, Carolyn. *Lucy Parsons: American Revolutionary* (Chicago, 1976).

Bailey, M. Thomas. *Reconstruction in Indian Territory: A Story of Avarice, Discrimination, and Opportunism* (Port Washington, 1972).

Bardolph, Richard. *The Negro Vanguard* (New York, 1959).

Belous, Russel E., ed. *America's Black Heritage* (Los Angeles, 1969) tells the tale of early African and Indian founders of Los Angeles.

Beniniato, Stefanie. "Popé, Pose-yemu, and Naranjo: A New Look at Leadership in the Pueblo Revolt of 1680." *New Mexico Historical Review*, Vol. 65 (October 1990).

Bontemps, Arna, and Jack Conroy. *Anyplace But Here* (New York, 1966) has chapters on Du Sable and Beckwourth.

Braun, Matthew. *Black Fox* (Greenwich, Ct., 1972) is a fictionalized account of the adventures of Britton Johnson with Kiowas and Comanches in 1864.

Brooks, James F. *Captives & Cousins: Slavery, Kinship, and Community in the Southwest Borderlands* (Chapel Hill, 2002).

———, ed. *Confounding the Color Line: The Indian-Black Experience in North America* (Lincoln, 2002).

Brown, Dee. *Bury My Heart at Wounded Knee: An Indian History of the American West* (New York, 1971).

Burton, Arthur. *Black Gun, Silver Star: The Life and Legend of Frontier Marshal Bass Reeves* (Lincoln, 2006).

Crockett, Norman L. *The Black Towns* (Lawrence, 1979). A highly useful study.

Davidson, David M. "Negro Slave Control and Resistance in Colonial Mexico, 1519–1650," *Hispanic American Historical Review*, Vol. 46, No. 3 (August 1966).

Debo, Angie. *A History of the Indians of the United States* (Norman, Okla., 1970) is an excellent summary history of Native American Nations that includes some material on black members.

Durham, Philip, and Everett L. Jones, *The Adventures of the Negro Cowboys* (New York, 1969) discusses black cowhands of the last frontier and particularly Cherokee Bill and Bill Pickett. It is written for students and includes photographs.

Ellison, Mary. "Black Perceptions and Red Images," *Phylon* XLIV, #1, 44–45.

Forbes, Jack D. *Black Africans and Native Americans* (London, 1988) is a basic and perceptive study of biracial contacts by the acknowledged authority.

Foreman, Grant. *The Five Civilized Tribes* (Norman, Okla., reprinted 1977) tells the story of the major Indian Nations after they were driven from their homes in the East to Oklahoma.

Foster, Laurence. *Negro Indian Relations in the Southeast* (Philadelphia, 1935) is a doctoral thesis which includes historical and field work data on Seminoles in Oklahoma, Texas, and Mexico.

———. "Negro Indian Relationships in the Southwest." Ph.D. Dissertation, University of Pennsylvania, 1935 (copy in author's possession).

Galeano, Eduardo. *Open Veins of Latin America: Five Centuries of the Pillage of a Continent* (New York, 1991).

Greene, Lorenzo J. *The Negro in Colonial New England, 1620–1776* (New York, 1942, reprinted 1968).

Hall, Gwendolyn Midlo. *Africans in Colonial Louisiana* (Baton Rouge, 1992) is the first thorough study of resistance to Spanish and French rule by Indians and Africans in Louisiana.

Harrington, Lonnie. *Both Sides of the Water: Essays on African-Native American Interactions* (Pittsburgh, 2007).

Katz, William Loren. *The Black West: A Documentary and Pictorial History of the African American Role in the Westward Expansion of the United States* (New York, 1996, Simon & Schuster edition, revised and expanded) includes information and photographs documenting the relationship between Africans and Native Americans on New World frontiers.

———. *Breaking the Chains: African American Slave Resistance* (New York, 1990). Several chapters detail resistance by enslaved Indians and Africans.

Landers, Jane. *Fort Mose: A Free Black Town in Spanish Colonial Florida* (St. Augustine, Florida, 1992) is based on archaeological and historical research in Spanish records.

Leckie, William H. *The Buffalo Soldiers* (Norman, Okla., 1967) is a scholarly study detailing the role of the buffalo soldiers on the last frontier.

Littlefield, Daniel F., Jr. *Africans and Seminoles: From Removal to Emancipation* (Westport, 1977) is a fine documented study.

Love, Edgar F. "Legal Restrictions on Afro-Indian Relations in Colonial Mexico," *Journal of Negro History*, Vol. LV, No. 2 (April 1970).

———. "Negro Resistance to Spanish Rule in Colonial Mexico," *Journal of Negro History*, Vol. LII, No. 2 (April, 1967).

Love, Nat. *The Life and Adventures of Nat Love* (New York, reprinted 1968) is the loud and proud story of a black cowhand who encountered Indians during the days of the great cattle drives.

Miles, Tiya, and Sharon P. Holland, eds. *Crossing Waters, Crossing Worlds: The African Diaspora in Indian Country* (Durham, 2006). A fine selection of recent and perceptive articles.

Miller, Loren. *The Petitioners: The Story of the Supreme Court of the United States and the Negro* (New York, 1967).

Minges, Patrick, ed. *Black Indian Slave Narratives* (Winston-Salem, 2004).

Mörner, Mangus. *Race Mixture in the History of Latin America* (Boston, 1967).

Mulroy, Kevin. *Freedom on the Border* (Lubbock, Tex., 1993) a valuable update of research by Porter on the Black Seminoles.

Nash, Gary B. *Red, White and Black: The Peoples of Early America* (Englewood Cliffs, New Jersey, 1974).

Opala, Joseph A. *A Brief History of the Seminole Freedmen* (Austin, Tex., 1980) is a summary written for students about the Black Seminole alliance that includes photographs, maps, and a chronology.

———. "Seminole-African Relations on the Florida Frontier," *Papers in Anthropology*, Vol. 22, No. 1 (Spring 1981) examines the complicated, changing relationship between the two races within the Seminole Nation from a new scholarly perspective.

Perdue, Theda. "Cherokee Planters, Black Slaves, and African Colonization," *Chronicles of Oklahoma*, Vol. 60, No. 3 (1982).

Porter, Kenneth Wiggins. *The Negro on the American Frontier* (New York, 1971) includes scholarly articles on relations between Africans and Native Americans from the earliest European explorations through the nineteenth century, with special focus on the Seminole Nation, the fur trade, and the southern United States before the Civil War.

———. *The Black Seminoles: History of a Freedom-Seeking People* (Gainesville, 1996).

Revised and edited by Alcione M. Amos and Thomas P. Senter. An updated version of a Porter manuscript.

Price, Richard. *First Time: The Historical Vision of an Afro-American People* (Baltimore, 1983) is an anthropological study of the Saramaka people of Surinam and their maroon history. It is the first effort at a thorough study of a maroon people who survived for centuries.

————, ed. *Maroon Societies* (New York, 1973) has scholarly articles on maroon societies in Latin America's Spanish, Portuguese, French, and Dutch colonies, including the Republic of Palmares in Brazil.

"Pursuing the Past in the Twenty-First Century," The Black Past, blackpast.org.

Shirley, Glen. *Law West of Fort Smith* (New York, 1957) tells the story of Judge Isaac Parker's frontier justice in the Indian Territory, with special emphasis on Cherokee Bill and the Rufus Buck gang.

Taylor, Quintard. *In Search of the Racial Frontier: African Americans in the American West, 1528–1990* (New York, 1998).

Vincent, Theodore G. *The Legacy of Vicente Guerrero: Mexico's First Black Indian President* (Gainesville, 2001).

Walton-Raji, Angela Y. *Black Indian Genealogy Research* (Maryland, 1993).

Weeks, William. *John Quincy Adams and American Global Empire* (Lexington, 1992).

Willis, William S. "Divide and Rule: Red, White, and Black in the Southeast," *Journal of Negro History,* Vol. XLVIII, No. 3, (July 1963).

Winston, Sanford. "Indian Slavery in the Carolinas Region," *Journal of Negro History,* Vol. XIX, No. 4 (October, 1934).

Wright, James L., Jr. *Creeks and Seminoles* (Lincoln, Nebraska, 1986).

INDEX

Jefferson, Thomas, 15–16, 106, 120, 229
Jesup, Sidney Thomas, 66–74
John Horse (Seminole)
    Indian Territory and, 77
    Mexico and, 78–80, 94
    oral petition of, 95–96
    Seminole wars and, 67, 70–72, 75
    Texas and, 82, 85, 87, 89–91
Johnson, Anthony, 111
Johnson, Britton, 216–218
Johnson, Bunk, 237
Johnson, Grant, 186
Johnson, James P., 237
Johnstone, James H., 112
Joliet, Louis, 127
Jones, Everett L., 3
Joss, John, 186
July, Maoma, 182

Kalm, Peter, 120
Katz, Ben, 237
Katz, William Loren, 3–4
Kearny (General), 137
Kickapoo Indians, 76, 78, 158
King, Johannes, 40
King, Martin Luther, Jr., 201, 232–233
"King" Fisher outlaw gang, 85, 90–91
Kiowa Indians, 83, 148, 203, 214, 217
Ku Klux Klan, 195, 198

Lake Okeechobee (battle), 73
Lakota Indians, 207, 233
Lane, Jim, 159–160
Langston, Charles, 239
Langston, John Mercer, 239
Las Casas (bishop), 27–28
Leary, Lewis Sheridan, 239
Lewis, Edmonia, 145–148
Lewis, Jake, 179

Lewis, Meriwether, 106
Lews and Clark expedition, 105–108
Lincoln, Abraham, 147, 158
Lipan Indians, 76, 148
Lisa, Manuel, 129–131
Lone Star Rebellion (Texas), 148
Lossing, Benson J., 10
Love, Nat, 204–205
Love, Robert, 186
Lowry, Henry Berry, 195

Madison, James, 14–15, 57, 59
Malcolm X, 235
Mandan Indians, 107
maroon settlements. *See also* Seminole
    Nation
    along Atlantic coast, 142–145
    equality of women in, 11–12, 45
    Gracia Real de Santa Teresa de Mose, 117
    guerrilla tactics, 12, 41, 46
    historical background, 11–15, 38–44
    important beliefs held by, 11, 30–31, 42
    independence movement in Mexico,
      50–52
    leaders and, 45–47
    Pee Dee River colony, 22–27
    Republic of Palmares, 47–50
    San Miguel de Gualdape, 24–26
    typical names, 11, 41
Marquette, Jacques, 127
Marshall, Marcia, 239
Matawai Indians (Guianas), 40
McCabe, Edwin P., 166–171
McIntosh (Chief), 58
Means, Russell, 233
Melungeon Indians, 143
Mendoza, Antonio de, 36, 101
Menendez, Francisco, 117
Mezzerow, Mezz, 237